Air Fryer QUEEN

STEPH DE SOUSA

STEPH DE SOUSA

For the original Queen, my sister Therese Alexander.
I know you're still watching from your palace in heaven.
"WE GOT THIS"

CONTENTS

The Fryer Club

GRAB YOUR BASKETS, FOODIES! THE AIR FRYER CLUB IS WHERE WE'RE FLIPPING THE FRY GAME ON ITS HEAD. WHERE WE'RE ALL ABOUT FUN, FLAVOUR AND FRYING. SO GET READY TO AIR FRY YOUR WAY TO DELICIOUSNESS!

Keep an eye out for these symbols on a recipe. They'll tell you at a glance if it's Vegetarian, Gluten Free or Freezer-friendly!

BUYING WISDOM

So you're on the hunt for the ultimate air fryer, huh? Well, strap in because I've got the lowdown for you! First off, size matters: are you cooking for one, two, or a whole hungry family? Pick a size that matches your needs. Next, make sure to peep those reviews! People love to share their crispy success stories (and cautionary tales). And don't forget about the features: do you need a digital display, preset cooking options, or maybe a rotisserie function? Finally, make sure it's easy to clean, because no one likes to scrub an oven!

WHAT CAN I COOK IN?

Let's talk air fryer containers. First rule of Fryer Club: always, ALWAYS check your user manual – don't want any surprise meltdowns, right? Generally, anything oven-safe can brave the air fryer arena. So, those silicone moulds, metal cake pans or oven-safe glass are all good to go! And those little disposable aluminium baking trays (4cm deep, 15.7cm x 21.9cm) are perfect for baking slices in. Just steer clear of anything melty or warpy, like most plastics. And give your container a little wiggle room; don't jam-pack it in there. You want that hot air to circulate and work its magic.

THE GO-GOS

Think of your air fryer like a mini oven but with so much more than an oven! If you can cook it in a regular oven, chances are it's going to be even better in your air fryer. Think roasted meats, juicy schnitty, crunchy chips, amazing roast potatoes, quick breakfasts, and super-fast reheats! If you love crispy and crunchy, the air fryer is your go-go!

TIPS AND TRICKS ON HOW TO CLEAN YOUR AIR FRYER

My most asked question after "What air fryer should I buy?", is "How do I clean my air fryer?" There are a few tricks that you can employ such as lining under the basket with baking paper or foil, if your air fryer is that style, to catch drips.

Spraying the basket lightly with oil can also make foods less likely to catch and make light work of cleaning. Check your manual, but all the air fryers I have used have been dishwasher safe.

My best advice is to treat it like a frying pan. Wash your air fryer basket after each use and you will avoid a build up of baked-on grime that is tough to get clean. If you have been a bit slack, I like to give it a soak in hot water with a dishwasher tablet. It will be clean in no time.

THE NO-NOS

Before you throw just ANYTHING into that magical machine, there are a few no-nos. Super wet batters? Nope, they'll just drip and make a mess before they can crisp up. I have never been able to cook rice or pasta! I have tried and tried but have failed every time! Popcorn was another one of my epic failures! Cakes are another tricky one. I have two recipes in this book that I have had success with, but about 100 other recipes have failed! Also, delicate, leafy greens just fly around like they're at a wild party instead of getting crispy. So, while your air fryer can perform kitchen miracles, it's not for everything.

TO PREHEAT OR NOT?

Do you need to preheat your air fryer? Ah, the age-old air fryer question! Here's the scoop: while many air fryers heat up super quickly and you can technically toss in your goodies without preheating, doing a quick warm-up (usually about 3-5 minutes) can help your food cook more consistently and crisply. Think of it as giving your fryer a little heads-up, like "Hey, we're about to rock the kitchen!" Some recipes might even specify preheating for the best results. But in a pinch? Skipping it isn't the end of the world. Just keep an eye on your food and maybe add a minute or two to the cooking time if needed. If I'm being honest, I very rarely preheat mine!

FAT MATTERS

Spray oil will be your new BFF when you start air frying. A little spritz on the base to prevent sticking and a light spray on top of your food for extra crispness will make your cooking even more amazing. My preference is always olive oil spray.

SAFETY FIRST

I don't need to preach to the converted but...Safety First!

These babies get HOT and I have the scars on my hands to prove it. My best advice is, DON'T TOUCH IT with bare hands EVER! It can be tricky to get your bakes out of that little basket but just be smart. A few quick tips to prevent frying your own hands:

- Always use an oven mitt or tongs.
- Let it cool for a few minutes before taking large things out.
- Remove the basket completely from your fryer so you have better access to your bake.

EVERY THING BREKKIE

MAKES 2

A DELICIOUS ANSWER TO LEFTOVERS: FRITTATA TOASTS

Here is your answer to the leftover nightmare in your fridge. Let your imagination go crazy with endless combos ripe for a second life. Think leftover roast, curry, bolognese, savoury mince!!

WHAT YOU NEED

4 EXTRA-LARGE EGGS

2 TBSP MILK OR CREAM

SALT AND PEPPER

1 CUP LEFTOVER ROAST VEGETABLES AND/OR MEAT

6 GRAPE OR CHERRY TOMATOES, HALVED

2 SLICES TASTY CHEESE

2 THICK SLICES WHITE OR WHOLEMEAL BREAD

OLIVE OIL COOKING SPRAY

WHAT YOU DO

Let's start the fun! Crack those eggs into a bowl and using a fork, mix them with your milk and a little salt and pepper until they're all blended and creamy. Next, find two dishes about the size of your bread (they can be square or round), then grease and line with baking paper. Divide this yummy mixture between the dishes.

Next, divide your leftovers and those cute little cherry tomatoes between the dishes, then crown the mix with a slice of cheese for your breakfast of champions.

Now, it's bread time! Plop your slice right on top of this scrumptious mixture and give it a gentle nudge.

It's cooking time! Give the bread a quick spray with oil then pop those dishes into your trusty air fryer and set the temperature to a cosy 170°C and the timer for 10 minutes.

And now, the golden moment! Once it's all crispy and a beautiful golden brown, carefully take it out, give it a flip and voilà!

You've just whipped up leftover frittata on toast. Perfect for breakfast or dinner, this dish will surely get you dancing in the kitchen!

PREP & COOK TIME 15 mins

STEPH
SAYS
REMEMBER, THERE IS
ALWAYS SOMEONE WHO
LIKES THE BURNT BITS.

STEPH
SAYS
PERFECTION IS OVERRATED. THOSE 'WHOOPS' MOMENTS ARE YOUR NEW RECIPE.

MAKES 1

FAST & FAB RICOTTA BLUEBERRY TORTILLA PIE

Easy, creamy, crunchy and a little bit sweet. If you like a sweet breakfast without the guilt, this one is just for you.

WHAT YOU NEED

- **2 TBSP RICOTTA**
- **1 REGULAR TORTILLA (20CM) (THAT FITS YOUR AIR FRYER BASKET)**
- **A SPRINKLING OF CINNAMON**
- **1 TSP BROWN SUGAR OR HONEY**
- **A HANDFUL OF BLUEBERRIES**
- **OLIVE OIL COOKING SPRAY**
- **TO SERVE: VANILLA YOGHURT AND HONEY**

WHAT YOU DO

First off, plop your ricotta right smack in the middle of your tortilla. It's gonna be the heart of your pie!

Then comes the cinnamon, sugar, or honey shower! Sprinkle it all over that lovely ricotta cheese. Sweetness and spice, everything nice!

It's blueberry time! Load up those gorgeous blue orbs on top.

Now, carefully fold the edges of your tortilla into the middle and give it a good roll. It's like wrapping a present, only tastier!

Finally, whisk it off into your air fryer and give the pie a quick spray with oil. Set the temperature to 180°C and the timer for a swift 8-minute bake. Then sit back, relax and wait for the magic to happen!

And voilà, you've just created a ricotta blueberry tortilla pie. Add yoghurt and a drizzle of honey and you're good to go!

PREP & COOK TIME 10 mins

CRISP POTATO PANCAKES WITH A CUMIN KICK

MAKES 12

WHAT YOU NEED

3 LARGE POTATOES (600G), COARSELY GRATED

2 GREEN ONIONS, FINELY CHOPPED

1 TSP CUMIN SEEDS OR GROUND CUMIN

⅓ CUP SELF-RAISING FLOUR

SALT AND PEPPER

OLIVE OIL COOKING SPRAY

WHAT YOU DO

Place grated potato in a sieve to drain. Then combine in a large bowl with green onions, cumin, flour, salt and pepper. Make sure you give it a good mix.

Line the base of your air fryer basket with baking paper and spray with oil spray.

Using a ¼-cup measuring cup, fill it with potato mixture and shake out into the air fryer basket. Repeat to make 4 pancakes then spray the tops with oil spray.

Set the temperature to 200°C and the timer for 5 minutes. Flip pancakes and spray with oil, then cook for another 5 minutes.

Repeat the process two more times with the remaining mixture to make 12 pancakes all up.

When they are done, sprinkle with a little salt! These are also amazing with sour cream and green onion or dipped into poached eggs!

PREP & COOK TIME 35 mins

BETTER-THAN-TOAST TORTILLA PIZZA

MAKES 1

WHAT YOU NEED

1 REGULAR TORTILLA (20CM) (THAT FITS YOUR AIR FRYER BASKET)

1 TBSP PIZZA SAUCE

¼ CUP GRATED CHEESE OF CHOICE

2 SLICES HAM, DICED

½ RED CAPSICUM, DICED

1 EXTRA-LARGE EGG

WHAT YOU DO

Start by placing your tortilla in your air fryer basket. Spread the pizza sauce all over your tortilla.

Sprinkle three-quarters of your grated cheese over the sauce. Add the ham and capsicum on top.

Gently crack the egg in the middle of your tortilla. Sprinkle the remaining cheese over your egg. Season.

Gently slide your basket into the air fryer and set the temperature to 180°C and the timer for 10 minutes; cook until the egg is set to your liking.

Slice it like a pizza so it feels more real! This is perfect for breakfast or dinner, and to get you dancing in the kitchen!

PREP & COOK TIME 15 mins

MAKES 2

CREAMY, DREAMY YOGHURT CUSTARD TOAST

I went diving deep into the TikTok trend pool with this one! The ever-viral custard toast. It's the whole package: quick, simple, oh-so-yummy, and filled with fun vibes. And honestly, dessert for breakfast? Sign. Me. Up!

WHAT YOU NEED

1 EXTRA-LARGE EGG

¾ CUP OF YOUR FAVOURITE YOGHURT

SPLASH OF VANILLA EXTRACT

1 TBSP HONEY OR SUGAR

2 X 3CM THICK SLICES BREAD

HANDFUL OF BERRIES

WHAT YOU DO

Mix together the egg, yoghurt, vanilla and honey in a bowl until you get a super sweet and creamy blend.

Here's the fun twist! Use an 8cm based glass, or even the back of a spoon, to press down and create a little hollow spot in the centre of your bread slices.

Pop your bread into the air fryer basket and carefully pour the yoghurt custard mixture into those hollow spots. Berry time! Sprinkle the top with some colourful, juicy berries of your choice.

Set the temperature to 170°C and the timer for 10 minutes. Let the magic happen!

When it's done, you'll have a toasty treat that's just waiting to be devoured!

PREP & COOK TIME 15 mins

STEPH
SAYS
LIFE'S TOO SHORT FOR
'PERFECT' DISHES. IT'S
THE QUIRKY, UNEXPECTED
TWISTS THAT MAKE
DISHES UNFORGETTABLE.

BONUS

Thou Shalt Spread the Gospel: Found the joy of the perfect crunch? Share it! Pop on over to Instagram and tag me in your Air Fryer creations.

THE TEN COMMANDMENTS

1 THOU SHALT NOT WORSHIP OTHER APPLIANCES

Listen up, dear kitchen enthusiast! Your air fryer is kinda like that friend who's a little jealous but also super awesome. It wants to make everything crispy and delicious without making you feel like you've sinned with too much oil. So, let's give it some love, okay?

2 THOU SHALT NOT FORGET TO SEASON

The air fryer kingdom is not one for bland meals. Think of seasoning as the magic touch. Forget it and you risk a meal that's as interesting as watching paint dry. So spice it up!

3 THOU SHALT NOT OVERCROWD

Here's the deal. You can't shove everything in and expect perfectly crispy results. Give your food some room to breathe. Let's "air" on the side of caution, shall we?

4 HONOUR THY TONGS

Think of tongs as your trusty sidekick. They keep your fingers safe and the food turning perfectly. So, be nice to them and they'll help you nab that perfect bite.

5 THOU SHALT NOT WASTE SOGGY LEFTOVERS

With the mighty air fryer, you can give that sad slice of pizza or droopy fry a second chance. Breathe new life (and crunch) into them!

6 THOU SHALT SHAKE IT OFF

Taylor wasn't just singing about ex-boyfriends. Give those fries or nuggets a good shake midway and watch them crisp up like a dream.

7 THOU SHALT USE LESS OIL

Remember, it's an air fryer, not an oil pool party. A little drizzle or a spritz is all you need to make things golden and gorgeous. Embrace less!

8 THOU SHALT CLEAN AFTER EVERY FRY

Leftover bits can be party poopers. They'll try to set off that noisy fire alarm. So, do yourself a favour and give it a quick clean. Your ears (and neighbours) will thank you.

9 REMEMBER, THE AIR FRYER IS NOT A MIRACLE WORKER

Yes, it's magical, but let's not get carried away. It's brilliant at some things but don't expect it to churn out frozen yoghurt or whip up a cappuccino.

10 SEEKETH NEW RECIPES

Don't let your air fryer game get old. Dive into those cookbooks and treat your taste buds to something new and exciting!

NOW, MY AIR FRYER CRUSADER, GO FORTH WITH YOUR AIR FRYER KNOWLEDGE AND MAY YOUR MEALS ALWAYS BE MOUTH-WATERINGLY DELICIOUS.

STEPH SAYS

MOST COOKING FAILS CAN BE RESCUED BY JUST SPRINKLING SOME CHEESE ON TOP.

MAKES 1

CREAMY & HEALTHY COTTAGE CHEESE OMELETTE

You can keep this omelette low carb and high protein, or do what I do and add a thick piece of buttered toast on the side.

WHAT YOU NEED

- **2 EXTRA-LARGE EGGS**
- **¼ CUP CREAMED COTTAGE CHEESE**
- **2 BUTTON MUSHROOMS, DICED**
- **1 TBSP CRUMBLED FETA**
- **½ GREEN ONION, THINLY SLICED**
- **SALT AND PEPPER**
- **TO SERVE: SLICED FRESH RED CHILLI, SLICED GREEN ONION AND CORIANDER LEAVES**

WHAT YOU DO

Grab a 1-cup ceramic ramekin (don't use metal or it will overcook) and beat the eggs and cottage cheese together until you get a silky, smooth texture.

Toss in the diced mushrooms, crumbled feta and sliced green onion. Sprinkle a pinch of salt and pepper to jazz things up.

Stir the mixture like a boss until everything is well mixed and the ingredients are best buddies.

Now, the fun part! Put your wonderful mix into the air fryer and set the temperature to a comfy 180°C and the timer for 10 minutes, then kick back and wait for the magic to unfold.

Eat this as it is or dress it up with a little freshness: sliced red chilli, sliced green onion and coriander.

PREP & COOK TIME 15 mins

MAKES 2

You can serve these beauties on buttered toast. Tuck 2 slices of thick-cut bread around the mushies in the air fryer. Slather the toast with butter then sit the mushrooms on top so it soaks up all the precious flavours.

CHEESY TWIST ON STUFFED MUSHROOMS

WHAT YOU NEED

- **2 LARGE WHITE FLAT MUSHROOMS**
- **2 EXTRA-LARGE EGGS**
- **½ CUP DICED HAM**
- **¼ CUP GRATED MOZZARELLA**
- **SALT AND PEPPER**
- **TO SERVE: BABY SPINACH LEAVES**

WHAT YOU DO

Clean your mushrooms by brushing off any loose dirt with paper towel and remove the stems, creating cute little mushroom cups.

Crack an egg into each mushroom, making sure not to spill any of that golden goodness.

Layer on some diced ham, adding a meaty twist to your creation.

Now, it's time for the cheese! Sprinkle your cheese on top, and a little salt and pepper too.

Let's get cooking! Grab your trusty air fryer and place the stuffed mushrooms inside.

Set the air fryer temperature to 180°C and the timer for 8 minutes, if you're craving a soft, dreamy egg that oozes deliciousness when you take a bite. For a firmer, heartier egg experience, go ahead and crank up the time to 10 minutes.

Once the timer goes off, carefully take out your stuffed mushrooms and serve with a handful of spinach.

PREP & COOK TIME 15 mins

STEPH
SAYS
SERVE THESE AS A
FANTASTIC BRUNCH
TREAT THAT'LL
IMPRESS EVERYONE
WHO TASTES THEM!

STEPH
SAYS
FOOD TASTES BETTER
WHEN YOU COOK IT
IN YOUR PYJAMAS.

MAKES 1

I don't need an excuse to eat cookies for breakfast, but if you do, this recipe is for you. The chocolate is optional but... you only live once.

BANANA & OAT COOKIE BAKED BLISS

WHAT YOU NEED

- **1 RIPE BANANA (THAT'S READY FOR MASHING)**
- **½ CUP ROLLED OATS**
- **A DASH OF CINNAMON**
- **1 TSP HONEY (OPTIONAL)**
- **3 SQUARES DARK CHOCOLATE (OPTIONAL)**

WHAT YOU DO

Let's start with your banana. Go ahead and mash it up really well. Make sure it's good and mushy.

Next, it's time to add your oats and cinnamon into the banana mash – stir 'em up until they're all friendly with each other.

If you're in the mood for a sweet little something, add in your honey. This is totally up to you!

After your ingredients are all mixed up, line your air fryer basket with some baking paper.

Now, take that delicious mix and plop it on the baking paper. Flatten it out until it's about the size of your coffee cup. Top with your chocolate squares.

Finally, it's time to bake this beauty! Pop it in the air fryer, set the temperature to 180°C and the timer for 7 minutes and there you have it!

PREP & COOK TIME 12 mins

HEALTHY-ISH BREAKFAST CAKES

MAKES 2

WHAT YOU NEED

- **1 CUP ROLLED OATS**
- **1 RIPE BANANA, MASHED**
- **2 TBSP PEANUT BUTTER**
- **1 TSP BAKING POWDER**
- **2 EXTRA-LARGE EGGS**
- **¼ CUP MILK**
- **½ CUP ADD-INS OF YOUR CHOICE (BERRIES, NUTS, SEEDS... WHATEVER FLOATS YOUR BOAT!)**

WHAT YOU DO

Grab a big bowl and mix all your ingredients together until they're best friends.

Now, share the love. Divide the mix between two 1-cup ramekins.

Ready for the magic? Slide the ramekins into an air fryer and set the temperature to 150°C and the timer for 20 minutes.

When the timer goes off, you've got a tasty breakfast masterpiece! Eat the brekkie cakes straight from the dishes.

To make these even more awesome, pop on some yoghurt, a couple of raspberries and a drizzle of honey.

PREP & COOK TIME 25 mins

POTS OF PANCAKES

MAKES 6

WHAT YOU NEED

1 EXTRA-LARGE EGG

1¾ CUPS MILK

SPLASH OF VANILLA

⅓ CUP CASTER SUGAR

2 CUPS SELF-RAISING FLOUR

TO SERVE: ICE-CREAM OR FROZEN YOGHURT AND A TOUCH OF HONEY

WHAT YOU DO

Start by combining your egg, milk, vanilla and sugar in a large mixing bowl. Give it a good whisk.

Add the flour and stir until you have a smooth batter. You don't want any lumps!

Pour your batter equally into six 1-cup ramekins (or other little dishes), filling each about half full. Don't be tempted to fill them to the top as the batter will rise and may overflow.

Now it's time for the air fryer. Place your ramekins in the basket. Set the temperature to 170°C and the timer for 15 minutes, and cook until the centre of your pancakes are firm.

And there you have it! Delicious, air fryer pancake pots, hot and ready to be enjoyed and topped with ice-cream and honey!

PREP & COOK TIME 20 mins

SAUSAGE & EGG MUFFINS WITHOUT THE MAC

MAKES 2

And just like that, you've got a quick, delicious, air-fried breakfast that's going to keep you powered all day!

WHAT YOU NEED

- 2 ENGLISH MUFFINS
- 2 BEEF OR PORK SAUSAGES
- 2 SMALL EGGS
- SALT AND PEPPER
- OLIVE OIL COOKING SPRAY
- 2 SLICES CHEESE (OPTIONAL, BUT WHO ARE WE KIDDING?)
- TO SERVE: TOMATO SAUCE

WHAT YOU DO

Split the muffins in half. Use the base of a glass to create a little nest in the muffin tops and remove some of the crumbs to make a little case.

Place your little muffin cases in the air fyer. Set the temperature to 190°C and the timer for 5 minutes until they're lightly toasted.

While that's ticking away, squeeze the meat from a sausage onto each muffin base and spread it out all the way to the edge as it will shrink back. This is going to be the tasty top for our egg!

Crack your eggs right into those comfy toasted muffin cases! Now, don't forget to sprinkle with salt and pepper for that extra kick!

Load the sausage-side bad boys into your air fryer basket, give your eggs a little spray with olive oil, and let the magic happen! Keep the temperature at 190°C and set the timer for 7 minutes or until the egg whites are set and the yolks are all gooey.

To finish, place the cheese on the egg muffin half (it'll melt into dreamy deliciousness!), then top with the sausage half and you are good to go. Oh, and don't forget the sauce!

PREP & COOK TIME 20 mins

STEPH
SAYS
I LIKE TO ADD A
DOLLOP OF TOMATO
SAUCE BECAUSE WHAT'S
A SAUSAGE WITHOUT
ITS BEST MATE, RIGHT?

STEPH
SAYS
REMEMBER THE COOK DOESN'T HAVE TO DO THE DISHES, SO IF YOU'RE NOT MAKING A MESS, ARE YOU EVEN COOKING?

MAKES 3

HEAVENLY FETA & EGG BREAKFAST PIES

The angels will sing when you bite into these pies, guaranteed. And if you are a breakfast prepper, you can make these ahead and simply reheat in your fabulous air fryer.

WHAT YOU NEED

2 CUPS BABY SPINACH LEAVES

¾ CUP GREEK YOGHURT

1 CUP SELF-RAISING FLOUR

100G FETA

3 EXTRA-LARGE EGGS

SALT AND PEPPER

OLIVE OIL COOKING SPRAY

1 TSP SESAME SEEDS

WHAT YOU DO

Start by placing your spinach in a heatproof bowl and pour over boiling water. Drain; cool those leaves under running water. Now, squeeze out the mositure.

Next, mix your Greek yoghurt and flour in a bowl into a deliciously doughy consistency.

Now, turn it out onto a floured bench and give it a good knead – it's a great stress-buster! But only for about a minute.

Cut your dough into three equal pieces. Time to get handsy! Flatten out two pieces with your fingers until each is the size of a 12cm side plate then create a little rim to contain your egg.

Line your air fryer basket with baking paper then carefully place the two flattened pieces of dough next to each other on top. Crumble a third of your scrumptious feta in the middle of each round. Top each with a third of the spinach and create a little hollow, then crack over a beautiful egg. Season with salt and pepper.

Spray the tops with oil. Set the temperature to 200°C and the timer for 15 minutes. TAADAA! You've got a Greek-inspired flatbread!

Repeat with the third piece of dough, and the remaining feta, spinach and egg. Sprinkle seeds over all your pies.

PREP & COOK TIME 35 mins

SWEET, SIMPLE & SCRUMPTIOUS

BREKKIE SPRING ROLLS

MAKES 4

Lay 4 regular (20cm) tortillas on a clean work surface. Next, using ⅓ cup spread of choice (Nutella, peanut butter, lemon curd, cream cheese, Biscoff, jam anyone?), slather 1 tbsp onto each tortilla. Top with sliced bananas, raspberries, blueberries or canned peaches – your choice! Fold in the sides then roll them up, nice and tight. Give them a spritz of olive oil spray then place your breakfast masterpieces into the air fryer. Set the temperature to 180°C and the timer for 5 minutes, cooking until golden brown.

PREP & COOK TIME 10 mins

STEPH
SAYS
NO MORE DULL BREAKFASTS WITH THESE SUPER DELICIOUS AND EASY BREAKFAST SPRING ROLLS!
LEMON CURD & BLUEBERRIES
CREAM CHEESE, PEACHES & CINNAMON SUGAR
PEANUT BUTTER & RASPBERRIES

MAKES 1

This is a speedy and satisfying breakfast treat that's a crowd-pleaser! Just pick a favourite filling; this could be crisp bacon, chorizo, sautéed veggies like pumpkin and carrot, or a mix of these things. Don't overthink it.

YOUR MORNING SAVIOUR: TORTILLA OMELETTE

WHAT YOU NEED

- 2 EXTRA-LARGE EGGS
- SALT AND PEPPER
- ½ CUP OF YOUR FAVOURITE FILLINGS (BACON, CHORIZO OR SAUTÉED PUMPKIN, JUST TO NAME A FEW!)
- ½ CUP GRATED CHEESE
- 1 REGULAR TORTILLA (20CM) (THAT FITS YOUR AIR FRYER)

WHAT YOU DO

First up, let's crack those eggs into a bowl. Sprinkle in some salt and pepper to season, and whisk it all up until it's smooth and perfectly blended.

Get your fillings ready. If you're using bacon, chorizo or veggies, make sure they're all finely chopped to a similar size.

Time to mix in your fillings and the cheese into the egg mixture, giving it a good stir to make sure everything's evenly spread out.

Now for the fun part! Pop your tortilla into an 18cm air fryer basket tray (or improvise and place in the air fryer basket). You're aiming for a tortilla bowl big enough to hold all the filling yumminess.

Pour your egg mixture into the tortilla bowl.

Now, set the temperature to a cosy 180°C and the timer for about 10 minutes. You're looking for a golden brown and crispy tortilla, and an omelette that's cooked to perfection.

Once everything's done, lift out the tray from the air fryer basket then carefully transfer your omelette to a plate. We wouldn't want to ruin our masterpiece, would we?

PREP & COOK TIME 15 mins

STEPH
SAYS
YOUR KITCHEN, YOUR RULES! IF YOU WANT TO PUT PINEAPPLE ON PIZZA, I SAY, "YOU DO YOU BOO."

STEPH
SAYS
MAKE SURE YOU LINE YOUR
AIR FRYER FOR THIS ONE
OR YOU WILL END UP WITH
A SLOPPY EGGY MESS IN THE
BOTTOM OF THE BASKET.

MAKES 1

CRACK A SMILE WITH EGG-CELLENT CHEESY BAGELS

You need to get on the Everything Bagel Seasoning train if you aren't already! It is the perfect savoury sprinkle that once you try it, you will put on everything.

WHAT YOU NEED

- 1 BAGEL
- 2 TBSP PESTO
- ½ CUP GRATED CHEESE (USE YOUR FAVOURITE)
- 2 EXTRA-LARGE EGGS
- SALT AND PEPPER
- 1 TSP EVERYTHING BAGEL SEASONING

WHAT YOU DO

Begin by slicing your bagel in half horizontally and spreading it generously with pesto.

Line the air fryer basket with baking paper. Use half your cheese to make a nice bed on the paper for your bagel halves. Place your bagel halves, pesto-side down on your cheese. Now, let's get cracking and break those eggs into the bagels' middle – put one egg in each round hole.

It's cheese time again! Shower your bagel and egg duo with the rest of the cheese.

Next up, we're adding some zing! Sprinkle your bagel halves with a pinch of salt and pepper to season. But wait, there's more! Add the Everything Seasoning, because, why not? It truly makes everything taste better!

Now, let's get cooking! Pop your creation into your air fryer and set the temperature to 200°C and the timer for 8 minutes.

As the timer goes off, get ready for the big reveal! Open your air fryer to be greeted by your delicious, crisp and golden pesto cheesy egg bagel.

PREP & COOK TIME 15 mins

QUICK & EASY DINNERS

SERVES 4

WINNER WINNER EASY CHICKEN DINNER

If you cook anything from this book, pleeeeeeeease cook this! It will be life changing, I promise. You have not had a Roast Chicken until you have cooked it in the air fryer.

WHAT YOU NEED

- 2 SMALL ONIONS
- 1 SMALL LEMON OR LIME
- 1 GARLIC BULB
- 1.5KG WHOLE CHICKEN
- OLIVE OIL, TO DRIZZLE
- SALT AND PEPPER

WHAT YOU DO

Quarter the onions and lemon, then halve the garlic bulb. Stuff the lemon and half the onion (the flavour-packed goodies), inside your chicken for a flavour party!

Drizzle some olive oil all over the chicken's skin, making sure it's well-coated – this will give it that irresistible golden crispiness.

Season your chicken generously with salt and pepper so every bite is bursting with flavour!

Place your chicken breast-side down in the air fryer. Set the temperature to 180°C and the timer for 60 minutes. After 30 minutes, flip your chicken over and place the rest of the onion and the garlic halves around the chicken.

Check your chicken to make sure it's cooked. Prick the fattest part of a thigh with a sharp knife. If the juice runs clear, it's cooked; if it's pink, pop it back in your air fryer for another 10 minutes.

Once your chicken is perfectly cooked and golden brown, set it aside to rest for a few minutes; it deserves a little break after all that sizzling! At the same time, reserve your onion and garlic to make a magic gravy!

Carve your chicken into beautiful portions, and don't forget the beautiful juices in the base of your fryer! Pour them over your chicken for extra tastiness.

PREP & COOK TIME
1 hr 15 mins

STEPH
SAYS
DIAL UP YOUR GRAVY
FLAVOUR BY BLITZING
THE RESERVED ONION
AND SQUEEZED GARLIC
INTO IT. MAGIC!

STEAMED CHICKEN BREAST FOR BUSY PEOPLE

SERVES 1

WHAT YOU NEED

- **1 CHICKEN BREAST**
- **SALT AND PEPPER**
- **OLIVE OIL, TO DRIZZLE**
- **½ TSP SPICE OF CHOICE (I LIKE CHILLI FLAKES/ POWDER OR DRIED BASIL)**

WHAT YOU DO

Take a piece of baking paper and plop your chicken breast right in the middle of it.

Now, let's make that chicken sing! Season it with a pinch of salt and pepper, and a drizzle of oil. Here's the fun part: toss in your spice if you're using it. This could be chilli flakes or chilli powder for a kick, or dried basil for an Italian vibe. The world is your oyster... Or in this case, your chicken!

Next, wrap up your little chicken package in the baking paper. Make sure it's well sealed so the flavours have a chance to mingle and get to know each other.

Pop your wrapped chicken into the air fryer and set the temperature to 200°C and the timer for 10-12 minutes. (The cooking time will vary a bit depending on how plump your chicken breast is. We want it cooked, but not overcooked!)

To check your chicken is done, prick it with a sharp knife, and if the juice runs clear, you're good to go! But if it's still a little pink, pop it back in the air fryer for a couple more minutes. And voilà! Serve with your favourite sides.

PREP & COOK TIME 20 mins

NEVER-LOOK-BACK AIR FRYER STEAK

SERVES 1

WHAT YOU NEED

- **YOUR FAVOURITE CUT OF BONELESS STEAK 2.5CM THICK**
- **OLIVE OIL, TO DRIZZLE**
- **SALT AND PEPPER**
- **SOME BUTTER**
- **TO SERVE: ONION RINGS**

WHAT YOU DO

Remove steak from the fridge and unwrap 30 minutes before cooking so the chill is gone.

I don't usually preheat the air fryer but for this recipe I do! Set the temperature to 200°C and the timer for 5 minutes.

Prep the steaks: Splash some olive oil on that bad boy, then shower it generously with salt and pepper, and rub in.

Toss your steak into the heated air fryer. Set the timer for 4 minutes. Now, flip that steak. Then, back into the air fryer it goes for another 4 minutes.

This timing is for medium-rare. For a medium steak, add 1 minute each side; for medium-well, add 2 minutes each side; and for well-done, add 3 minutes each side.

Alright, your steak's cooked. Now, quickly wrap it up in some foil with a little dollop of butter. Let it rest for 5 minutes. This lets all those tasty juices soak back into the steak, making it extra juicy and delicious.

Serve it up and enjoy your scrumptious steak with a side of onion rings!

PREP & COOK TIME 15 mins

SERVES 4

UNBELIEVABLE SOUTHERN ROASTED CHICKEN

Chicken was created for the air fryer, I'm sure of it! With this winning spice combination and the magic of the air fryer, you will kick fried chicken to the curb.

WHAT YOU NEED

- 1 TBSP SMOKED PAPRIKA
- 1 TSP ONION POWDER
- 1 TSP GARLIC POWDER
- 1 TSP CELERY SALT
- 1 TSP CHICKEN STOCK POWDER
- 4 CHICKEN THIGH CUTLETS
- OLIVE OIL, TO DRIZZLE
- TO SERVE: AÏOLI AND CORIANDER LEAVES

WHAT YOU DO

Grab a small bowl and throw in all your spices and the stock powder. Give it a good mix. This concoction right here is your ticket to flavourville, my friends.

Next, coat your chicken thighs with olive oil. Imagine you're painting a beautiful golden sunset, only this one is super yummy!

Now, it's time to let the magic dust work its wonders. Sprinkle the spice mix over your chicken and give it a nice rub. Let's show that chicken some love!

Lastly, it's time for our wonderful little kitchen helper, the air fryer! Pop your chicken in there, skin-side up, then set the temperature to 200°C and the timer for 18 minutes. Let the air fryer work its magic.

And there you have it! Crunchy, tasty chicken that's gonna jazz up your dinner time, ready to be drizzled with aïoli and topped with coriander.

PREP & COOK TIME 25 mins

DINNER
DATE
SERVE WITH MEXICAN
CORN FIESTA, PAGE 72.

THAT BREAD AIN'T DEAD

Unless it's mouldy, don't waste bread or tortillas; instead, wake and shake them up in the air fryer. For whole loaves, splash them with water and wrap in foil, or for stale slices, place as is in the air fryer for 3-5 mins. Hey presto, my friend, a new bakery-fresh loaf is born!

CROÛTONS + DIPPERS

Raid your pantry and fridge for tortillas and bread; cut into wedges, rounds or cubes, spray with a little oil, then toast in your magic machine at 180°C for 6-8 mins or until those little guys are sunbaked. Now, go add a flavour bomb to those crunchy morsels and rain over your choice of flavoured salts (see page 92).

CHEESE SCRAP FONDUE

Round up random packets of grated cheese, tragic-looking pieces of parmesan or other cheese scraps; grate, chop or slice then combine. Spread a generous amount of pesto to cover the base of a ramekin dish then add your combined cheesy goodness. Air fry at 180°C until gooey.

PUTTIN' POUTINE ON THE MAP

Never heard of it?! Okay... this Canadian food masterpiece of delectable fries, gravy and cheese is my inspo for dinner for fusspots. Line your air fryer basket with a piece of foil, making sure it comes up the sides a little bit too. Next up, add in your just-made Perfect Chips at Home (page 90), spreading them out so the base is covered, then scatter over chunky cubes of mozzarella. Now this is the point where you can go rogue on tradition: top it with handfuls of shredded chicken, chopped bacon or bits of ham. Let it all get toasty in the air fryer at 190°C for 10 mins until you've got a melty mound. All that's left is to souse the lot with a cheat's gravy!

$AVE ENERGY

That air fryer of yours can halve the cooking time of some foods that would chew up more energy if cooked in the oven. Prick jacket potatoes and microwave for 10 mins, then make them crispy by finishing your spuds off in the air fryer.

MAKE IT! DON'T BUY IT!

A 1kg bag of frozen chippies costs close to the same amount as a 4kg bag of spuds, so with a quick chop you can put money back into your wallet by making your own, plus you'll save on energy cooking them in the air fryer. And the best bit, you'll think you are a genius – home-made always wins!

ACE THE VEGGIES

Veggies typically cost less than meat and can be taken from boring to brilliant. Think carrots, zucchini, broccolini, eggplant or cauli. Cut into finger-sized pieces or cubes, add a glug of oil, then spices, fresh or dried herbs, salt and pepper. Tumble together and air fry for approx. 10 mins, giving them a shake halfway.

BEST EVER LEFTOVERS

Ditch the sog for crisp. You can reheat bread, pizza and pastries faster and smarter than the microwave and return them all to last night's dinner glory in minutes.

DITCH THE TAKEAWAY

Turn leftover rice into a cheat's fried rice with a few choice chopped leftover (or frozen) veggies. Toss through a flavour boost of soy sauce, five spice powder and sesame oil. Or pop last night's ravioli or spag into an air-fryer-friendly container, beat up a few eggs with some cheese and pour it over your pasta. Add in some little extras – hello ham and bacon! Air fry at 190°C for 25 mins until crispy.

DIY DESSERTS

Banana boats – split bananas in their skins lengthways, then pack with your choice of mini marshmallows, chopped chocolate bars or chips, crumbled Biscoff biscuits and/or strawberries. Wrap in foil, air fry at 190°C for 12 mins or until melty. More is more! Add caramel sauce, warmed Nutella or ice-cream, or add the lot!

CHEESY GOODNESS

A really good super cheesy toastie ticks lots of boxes. Choose mozzarella for stretch then add smoked cheddar, vintage cheddar or blue cheese for a flavour bang. Butter your bread, then pop into the air fryer at 180°C for 5 minutes. Spread with a little Dijon and pile cheese on one slice then top with the other. Air fry for 3-5 mins or until it's melted to gooey heaven.

ULTIMATE TOASTIE WITH THE LOT

Spread 2 thick slices of your favourite bread with mayo, then layer up one of them with goodies from the fridge. Start with a savoury spread, chutney or sauce, then pile on chopped-up leftover roast meat, savoury mince or sliced sandwich meat (be creative, folks, with what you've got – canned beans work well too!). Next, add leftover veggies and crown the layers with a mountain of cheese. Top it off with the other slice of bread, then pop your ultimate toastie in the air fryer at 180°C for 10 mins. Don't forget to flip it halfway so both sides are golden!

STEPH'S

Savvy Savers

STEPH
SAYS
COOKING IS LIKE HAVING A TODDLER AROUND: ALWAYS MESSY, OFTEN UNPREDICTABLE, BUT ALWAYS WORTH IT!

SERVES 4

Get ready for a flavour explosion of spicy, crunchy, irresistible chicken! You can make this meek and mild or mind-blowingly hot. You drive this bus.

EPIC CRISPY CHILLI CHICKEN

WHAT YOU NEED

- 1 TSP GARLIC POWDER
- 1 TSP ONION POWDER
- ¼ CUP CORNFLOUR
- 2 TBSP SESAME OIL
- 2 TBSP DARK SOY SAUCE
- 500G CHICKEN THIGH FILLETS, DICED
- OLIVE OIL COOKING SPRAY
- 1 LONG RED CHILLI, SLICED FINELY
- 2 GREEN ONIONS, SLICED FINELY
- 1 TSP SESAME SEEDS
- TO SERVE: MICROWAVE WHITE RICE

FOR THE STICKY SAUCE:

- ¼ CUP CHILLI OIL
- ¼ CUP HONEY
- ¼ CUP DARK SOY SAUCE
- CHILLI FLAKES (OPTIONAL)

WHAT YOU DO

Start off by mixing the garlic powder, onion powder and cornflour in a big zip-top bag.

Next, combine the sesame oil and soy sauce then toss in your chicken pieces, give it all a good stir making sure every piece gets a nice coat of the mixture.

Throw your chicken in the zip-top bag and give it a really good shake, coating your chicken all over in the flour mix.

Now, spray your air fryer basket with some olive oil, then place your chicken pieces in the basket. Make sure they're not all clumped together. Depending on the size of your air fryer, you might need to cook these in batches. Give your chicken a spray of olive oil.

Pop your chicken in the air fryer. Set the temperature to 200°C and the timer for 10-12 minutes, or until they're fully cooked. Give them a shake halfway through so every piece gets crispy.

While the chicken is getting all crispy and delicious, let's make the sticky sauce. Grab a largish pan and add the chilli oil, honey and soy sauce, and bring it to a sizzle over medium heat. Toss in your chilli flakes, if you're using them.

Once the chicken is cooked, add it to your sizzling sticky sauce and stir well so every piece is nicely coated.

For the finishing touch, sprinkle over the sliced fresh chilli, green onions and sesame seeds.

Voilà! Your air fryer crispy chilli chicken is ready to be devoured over warmed-up microwave rice. Enjoy your meal!

PREP & COOK TIME 25 mins

LET'S ROCK THIS AIR FRYER BUTTER CHICKEN!

WHAT YOU NEED

FOR TANDOORI CHICKEN:

- 1 TBSP GARLIC PASTE
- 1 TBSP GINGER PASTE
- 1 TBSP SMOKED PAPRIKA
- 1 TSP GROUND FENUGREEK (OPTIONAL, BUT YOU'LL LOVE IT!)
- 1 TSP GROUND CARDAMOM
- 1 TSP SALT
- 1 TSP PEPPER
- ½ CUP GREEK YOGHURT
- 6 CHICKEN THIGH FILLETS

FOR THE BUTTER CHICKEN SAUCE:

- 400G CAN DICED TOMATOES
- ½ CUP GREEK YOGHURT
- 1 TBSP GARLIC PASTE
- 1 TBSP GINGER PASTE
- 2 TSP GARAM MASALA
- 1 TSP GROUND CARDAMOM
- 1 TSP SMOKED PAPRIKA
- 100G COLD SALTED BUTTER, CHOPPED
- 1 TSP CASTER SUGAR

SERVES 4

Let the chicken hang out in the marinade for at least 30 minutes, or if you have more time, up to 24 hours. The longer it sits, the more flavourful it will be. You can go two ways with this recipe: simply make the tandoori chicken, or go next level and make the sauce to turn that into the most incredible butter chicken.

WHAT YOU DO

For tandoori chicken, let's start with mixing the garlic, ginger, all our yummy spices, salt, pepper and yoghurt together really well in a big bowl. Add your chicken and stir well so they are coated all over.

Next, let the chicken hang out in the marinade for at least 30 minutes or up to 24 hours, in the fridge of course.

Once your chicken has soaked up all that yummy marinade, let's cook it. Line your air fryer basket with baking paper, then pop those marinated chicken thighs on top. Set the temperature to 200°C and the timer for 20 minutes. Don't forget to flip them halfway through so they cook evenly and come out nice and golden and cooked through.

That's it, easy peasy! You've just made a delicious tandoori chicken.

Time to mix the butter chicken sauce if you are going there! Take a bowl, add in your tomatoes, yoghurt, garlic, ginger and spices. Add in any resting juices from the tandoori chicken and give it a good stir. Pop it in your microwave and heat for 2 minutes.

Slice up the cooked tandoori chicken. Now, add them to your delicious, fragrant, warm sauce.

Find an air-fryer-friendly dish (just make sure it fits!) and pop your butter chicken mix in there. Set the temperature to 200°C and the timer for 20 minutes. Remember to give it a stir every 5 minutes.

Time to bring in our buttery friend! Add your cold butter and the sugar to the mix, then stir until it's all melted and you've got a lovely, glossy sauce.

Serve your butter chicken hot, straight from the air fryer!

PREP & COOK TIME
1 hr (+ marinating)

DINNER DATE

SERVE YOUR BUTTER CHICKEN WITH FLUFFY MICROWAVE BASMATI RICE AND A DELICIOUS FLATBREAD LIKE NAAN OR PARATHA AND A SCATTERING OF CORIANDER AND YOU'RE GOOD TO GO!

LET'S ROCK THIS AIR FRYER BUTTER CHICKEN!

STEPH
SAYS
PILE YOUR SPICY CHICKEN
INTO WARMED TORTILLAS
WITH SLICED CUCUMBER
AND AVOCADO, PLUS A GOOD
DOLLOP OF SOUR CREAM
AND DRIZZLE OF HOT SAUCE.

SERVES 4

Say yes to a mid-week fiesta! Try these fajitas with chicken, rump steak, or even cauli. Whatever you fancy, it's all delish! Mix it up and munch on!

SPICE-IT-UP CHICKEN FAJITAS

WHAT YOU NEED

1 TBSP GROUND CUMIN

1 TBSP SMOKED PAPRIKA

1 TBSP DRIED OREGANO

1 TSP ONION SALT

1 TSP GARLIC POWDER

1 TSP GROUND CINNAMON

1 TSP SALT

½ TSP PEPPER

4 CHICKEN THIGH FILLETS, CUT INTO FINGER-SIZED PIECES

2 MEDIUM RED CAPSICUMS, SLICED

2 MEDIUM ONIONS, SLICED

OLIVE OIL, TO DRIZZLE

WHAT YOU DO

Gather all your spices, salt and pepper and put them in a large bowl and give them a good mix.

Grab your chicken pieces and plop them in the bowl with your spices. Get your hands in there and massage those spices into your chicken until they're thoroughly coated.

Add your sliced capsicums and onions to the same bowl. Give everything a good mix so the veggies get some of that spice love too.

Drizzle a generous amount of olive oil over your spiced chicken and veggies. Give them another good mix to ensure everything is well coated.

Once they're ready, transfer your spiced chicken and veggies into the air fryer. Set the temperature to 200°C and the timer for 25 minutes. Make sure to give your chicken a shake or turn them over to ensure they cook through evenly.

PREP & COOK TIME 30 mins

SERVES 4

The first step to achieving crackly pork is planning. If possible, snag your pork belly a day in advance and let it chill, uncovered, in the fridge. It's all about the dryness factor here, peeps! Don't worry if you don't do it, as your pork belly will still taste fantastic.

CRACKLING GOOD PORK BELLY WITH CHINESE FIVE SPICE

WHAT YOU NEED

- **1KG PIECE SCRUMPTIOUS BONELESS PORK BELLY, SKIN SCORED**
- **1 TBSP SEA SALT FLAKES**
- **1 TSP CHINESE FIVE SPICE**
- **1 TSP GROUND WHITE PEPPER**
- **TO SERVE: STEAMED GAI LAN WITH A SPLASH OF GLUTEN-FREE SOY SAUCE**

WHAT YOU DO

When it's time to get cooking, pat your pork belly dry with some paper towels. Make sure it's as dry as a summer's day in the desert.

Next, you're gonna take the salt, Chinese five spice and white pepper and mix them all together. This little spice mix is gonna make your pork taste like it's been on a holiday in the east!

Rub that flavourful spice blend all over your pork. Get into every nook and cranny, and don't forget the skin!

Now it's foil time! Wrap up your pork in foil but keep the top uncovered. This trick keeps your meat moist and juicy but still lets the skin get that awesome crispy texture.

Pop your wrapped-up pork into your air fryer. Set the temperature to 180°C and the timer for 60 minutes.

Once your air fryer dings, lift your pork out and give it a little rest. Let it sit for about 10 minutes before you dive in. Patience is a virtue, my friend, as it pays off with incredibly tender pork. Last but not least, don't forget to pour those delicious pan juices all over your pork. Trust me, it's a flavour bomb that takes your pork to the next level. Pair it on the plate with gai lan.

PREP & COOK TIME

1 hr 5 mins (+ resting)

STEPH
SAYS
STOP! HEAR ME OUT. YES, BOILED BRUSSELS SPROUTS IN THE 70S AND 80S WERE REVOLTING AND DESERVE THE HATE. BUT WE CAN TAKE THESE LITTLE GREEN NUGGETS FROM YUCK TO YUM!

SERVES 2

SWEET & SPICY PORK WITH YUM BRUSSELS SPROUTS

A little bit of spice makes everything nice, and these 3 little additions of brown sugar, garam masala and chilli powder turns your pork chops into a gourmet delight.

WHAT YOU NEED

- 1 TBSP BROWN SUGAR
- 1 TBSP GARAM MASALA
- 1 TSP CHILLI POWDER (OPTIONAL, BUT IT DOES GIVE A NICE KICK!)
- 2 TSP SALT
- 2 PORK CHOPS WITH THE BONE
- OLIVE OIL, TO DRIZZLE

FOR YUM BRUSSELS SPROUTS:

- 2 GRANNY SMITH APPLES
- 2 CURED CHORIZO SAUSAGES
- 500G BRUSSELS SPROUTS
- 1 TSP SALT
- ½ TSP PEPPER
- TO SERVE: RAITA

WHAT YOU DO

Start by mixing up your spice rub. In a bowl, toss in your brown sugar, garam masala, chilli powder (if you're using it) and salt. Give it a good mix until everything's well combined. This magic dust will turn ordinary pork chops into a carnival of flavours!

Next, it's time to dress up your pork chops. Cover them with olive oil. This will not only make them sizzle but also help your spice rub to stick perfectly.

Now, rub that aromatic spice rub all over your chops. Make sure you cover every nook and cranny so every bite is filled with taste.

Let's get them cooking! Pop your chops into your air fryer. Set the temperature to 200°C and the timer for 12 minutes. Don't forget to flip them halfway through for even cooking.

While that's cooking, get onto those yum Brussels sprouts: chop up your apples and the chorizo sausages into bite-sized pieces.

With the Brussels sprouts, you'll want to slice each one lengthways in 4. Gather your chopped ingredients in a bowl, ready for a seasoning shower. Sprinkle over the salt and pepper, then drizzle with more olive oil; you need a good amount. Mix everything together like it's a colourful food party; they should all be well coated with the oil and seasoning.

Once the chops are done, cover them with foil and give them a rest. They will be even more juicy and tender. Plus, it gives you time to cook the Brussels sprouts!

Put your sprout party mix in the air fryer. Set the temperature to 200°C and the timer for 15 minutes. Do a little happy shake dance with your air fryer basket halfway through!

Now, tuck in and enjoy these spectacular pork chops with a little raita and the most yum Brussels sprouts ever!

PREP & COOK TIME 40 mins

SERVES 4

DELICIOUSLY STICKY PORK BELLY BITES

The perfect sticky pork belly bites to share with friends and family... Or shush... to keep all to yourself!

WHAT YOU NEED

- **1KG PIECE BONELESS, SKINLESS PORK BELLY**
- **OLIVE OIL, TO DRIZZLE**
- **1 TBSP SMOKED PAPRIKA**
- **1 TSP ONION POWDER**
- **1 TSP GARLIC POWDER**
- **1 TSP SALT**
- **1 TSP PEPPER**

FOR THE STICKY SAUCE:

- **2 TBSP HONEY**
- **2 TBSP CHILLI SAUCE (FRANK'S HOT SAUCE WORKS A CHARM)**
- **2 TBSP BUTTER**

TO SERVE: CORIANDER

WHAT YOU DO

Chop up that pork belly into bite-sized pieces, and drizzle them with olive oil until they're all shiny and ready to cook.

Combine all the spices: smoked paprika, onion powder and garlic powder with the salt and pepper. Then, give your pork belly pieces a good rub-down with the spice mix. Make sure every piece is covered in delicious flavour!

Arrange your spiced pork belly pieces in your air fryer in one layer. Don't worry if you can't fit them all at once, you can always do a second round.

Set the temperature to 200°C and the timer for 25 minutes, then cook those bad boys, giving them a shake halfway through to ensure even cooking.

While your pork is sizzling away, get started on the sticky sauce: combine honey, chilli sauce and butter in a microwave-safe bowl big enough to toss your cooked pork belly in. Zap this in the microwave for 1-2 minutes or until butter is melted and sauce is gooey. Give it a stir to make sure it's all mixed together.

When your pork belly bites are crispy and golden, toss them in the sticky sauce bowl. Make sure each bite is coated with the yummy sauce! Then finish it off with coriander freshness.

And there you go, the perfect sticky pork belly bites to share with friends and family... Or not!

PREP & COOK TIME 40 mins

STEPH
SAYS
NOTHING WILL
EVER REPLACE REAL
BUTTER IN A RECIPE.

STEPH
SAYS
THE CHILLIES IN THIS
RECIPE ARE OPTIONAL,
BUT TRUST ME, IT'S
LIP-SMACKINGLY GOOD
WITH THEM!

SERVES 4 GENEROUSLY

Play food detective to track down the flavour mysteries in your dish. Too bland? Salt to the rescue! Too tangy? Add a pinch of sugar! A bit flat, add a squeeze of lemon or a dash of vinegar. All fixed.

NOT-YOUR-AVERAGE PUMPKIN CURRY SOUP

WHAT YOU NEED

- **1KG KENT PUMPKIN**
- **2 MEDIUM POTATOES**
- **½ CUP OLIVE OIL**
- **2 TBSP CURRY POWDER**
- **1 TBSP GARLIC PASTE**
- **1 TBSP GINGER PASTE**
- **2 TSP SALT**
- **1 LITRE STOCK (CHICKEN IS MY PERSONAL FAVE!)**
- **2 LONG GREEN CHILLIES (THESE ARE OPTIONAL)**
- **1 CUP GREEK YOGHURT**
- **TO SERVE: CORIANDER LEAVES**

WHAT YOU DO

Peel pumpkin and potatoes and chop them into sizable chunks. Plop them into a big bowl.

It's time for some flavour magic! Sprinkle your chunks with ¼ cup of the olive oil, the curry powder, garlic, ginger and salt. Give it a good ol' mix to make sure your veggies are coated in yumminess.

Into the air fryer they go and you'll need to keep the bowl! Set the temperature to 200°C and the timer for 30 minutes. Don't forget to give them a little shake halfway through for an even cook. You may need to do this in two batches.

While our chunky friends are getting roasty, heat up your stock. And for some fun, slice up your chillies, if you're game.

After the air fryer dings, toss your roasty chunks back in your original bowl. We don't want to lose any of those delicious flavours now, do we?

Time for the pour-over. Drench your chunks in the hot stock and whip out your stick blender. Get blitzing until it's soooooo smooth.

Add your remaining ¼ cup olive oil, blitz again and watch that soup become glossy and delish.

Ladle your soup into bowls, pop a dollop of Greek yoghurt on top then sprinkle with the sliced chilli and your fresh coriander. Voilà! A heartwarming bowl of flavourful goodness!

PREP & COOK TIME 40 mins

SERVES 4

Think classic roast potatoes are peak perfection? Well, think again! Here's a twist to elevate it. Because, let's be real, what spud doesn't get even better with a dollop of flavoured butter?!

BLOW YOUR MIND CHEESY POTATOES

WHAT YOU NEED

- **4 MEDIUM POTATOES (AND DON'T FORGET TO PEEL THEM!)**
- **OLIVE OIL, TO DRIZZLE**
- **1 TSP SALT**
- **2 TBSP BUTTER, MELTED**
- **FINELY GRATED ZEST OF 1 LEMON**
- **¼ CUP FINELY GRATED PARMESAN**

WHAT YOU DO

First things first, chop up your potatoes into big bite-size hearty pieces, then soak them in some cold water for about 10 minutes.

Once they've had their little bath, drain them and pat them dry using some paper towel. We don't want soggy spuds now, do we?

Now, get a bowl ready, plop in your potatoes, splash over some olive oil and sprinkle them with the salt. Give them a really good mix so they're all nice and coated.

Next, pop these potatoes into your air fryer. Set the temperature for 200°C and the timer for 25 minutes. Halfway through, give them a shake so they get evenly cooked.

While your taters are getting crispy, mix up your melted butter, lemon zest and cheese in a bowl. Get it all nice and combined.

When your potatoes are all cooked up and ready to meet their cheesy fate, plop them into your cheese mixture. Toss 'em and turn 'em until they're all coated in that delicious, tangy, cheesy butter!

And there you have it! Your new favourite side dish!

PREP & COOK TIME

35 mins (+ soaking)

STEPH'S VARIATIONS

Chicken Forget the lemon zest and cheese and instead add 2 tsp chicken stock powder to the butter for this flavour bomb!

Miso Forget the lemon zest and cheese and instead whisk 1 tbsp white (shiro) miso into the butter until smooth.

STEPH
SAYS
TO FINISH OFF THESE
LITTLE GREEN STICKS
OF LOVELINESS,
SHOWER THEM WITH
LEMON ZEST CURLS.
IF YOU DO, ZEST THE
LEMON BEFORE YOU
JUICE IT. TRUST ME!

SERVES 4

ZESTY LEMON & COCONUT GREEN BEANS

Boring Beans be Gonski. These are the new It girl in our house. These beans make everything taste better, but try them beside a curry for the perfect combo.

WHAT YOU NEED

500G GREEN BEANS, TRIMMED

¼ CUP SHREDDED COCONUT

JUICE OF 1 LEMON

1 TSP SALT

TWIST OF GROUND BLACK PEPPER

OLIVE OIL, TO DRIZZLE

WHAT YOU DO

Start by combining your green beans, shredded coconut, the juice of that bright lemon, the salt, a twist of black pepper and a good amount of olive oil in a big, happy bowl.

Give it a good mix until every bean is wearing a nice coat of the mixture.

Now, it's time for our air fryer to do its magic. Scrunch up a little bit of baking paper and line the air fryer basket. Take this deliciously dressed-up green bean mixture and pop it into your basket.

Set the temperature to 180°C and the timer for 12-15 minutes or until the beans are tender and the coconut is sun-kissed. Don't forget to give them a good shake halfway through.

And there you have it, your delicious coconut beans.

PREP & COOK TIME 20 mins

SERVES 4

Corn is a pain to cut! I like to keep my corn in its husk, run it under the tap, then pop it in the microwave for 2 minutes to make it super easy to cut through that tough centre core.

MEXICAN CORN FIESTA

WHAT YOU NEED

- **1 CUP MAYONNAISE**
- **2 TBSP SMOKED PAPRIKA**
- **1 TSP SALT**
- **½ TSP PEPPER**
- **GRATED ZEST AND JUICE OF 1 LIME**
- **3 COBS CORN, HUSKS REMOVED, QUARTERED LENGTHWAYS**
- **½ CUP FINELY GRATED PARMESAN**

WHAT YOU DO

In a bowl, combine mayonnaise, smoked paprika, salt, pepper, lime zest and juice. Give it a good mix until everything becomes best friends.

Time to pamper the corn: coat those corn pieces in your amazing mixture. Oh, and keep ⅓ cup of that mix aside for dipping; you'll thank me later!

Line your air fryer basket with baking paper and pop your corn in. Set the temperature to 200°C and the timer for 8 minutes or until they turn into a crispy golden delight. Don't forget to shake them halfway through.

The grand finale: now for the magical touch! Sprinkle that parmesan over your corn. Because cheese makes everything better, right? And don't forget the reserved mayo mixture for dipping; you'll want to give that a sprinkle of cheese too. And there you go! A taste extravaganza just waiting to be devoured.

PREP & COOK TIME 25 mins

STEPH
SAYS
A PINCH OF THIS,
A DASH OF THAT.
EXPERIMENT WITH
SPICES! SOMETIMES,
THE SECRET
INGREDIENT REALLY
IS A SPRINKLE OF
SMOKED PAPRIKA.

STEPH
SAYS
MAKE SURE YOU
"SHAKE IT BABY"
HALFWAY THROUGH
COOKING SO YOUR
MEATBALLS ARE
GOLDEN ALL OVER.

MAKES 16

THE ULTIMATE CROWD-PLEASING LEMONY LAMB MEATBALLS

It took me years of nagging to get this recipe from my friend Matt, and he will probably kill me for sharing it. His recipe is cooked in his fabulous pizza oven, so I can claim this version, right?

WHAT YOU NEED

500G LAMB MINCE

½ CUP PANKO BREADCRUMBS

2 TSP GROUND CUMIN

½ TSP PEPPER

1 TSP BEEF STOCK POWDER

1 MEDIUM POTATO

2 LEMONS

¼ CUP FINELY GRATED PARMESAN

OLIVE OIL COOKING SPRAY

TO SERVE: YOGHURT, PARSLEY, LEMON WEDGES AND PITA BREAD

WHAT YOU DO

Get a big bowl and put the lamb, breadcrumbs, spices and stock powder inside.

Now, it's time to get physical. Grab a grater and grate your potato on the side with the coarse holes directly over the mixture in the bowl. Time for some sunshine. Grate the lemons on the side with fine holes, also over the mixture, then add your cheese. Now get your hands in there and mix it up real good. We want every meatball to be a flavour party.

Roll the mixture into balls, each about 2 tablespoons in size. Think of making tiny edible snowballs!

Give your air fryer plate a good spray with olive oil. Now, place your meatballs in a single layer in the air fryer and give them a little spray of oil too. They will love it.

To cook those beauties, set the temperature to 200°C and the timer for 15 minutes. Halfway through, turn the meatballs over and give them another spray of olive oil. They are sunbathing in your air fryer!

For the finishing touches, drizzle the meatballs with tangy yoghurt and rain down some parsley. Serve them with lemon wedges and pita bread. Go eat!

PREP & COOK TIME 25 mins

COMFORT IN A BOWL OF TOMATO SOUP WITH GIANT CROUTONS

SERVES 4

Enjoy this warm bowl of deliciousness on any cold day or when you just need some good old comfort food.

WHAT YOU NEED

- 1 MEDIUM RED ONION
- 1 MEDIUM RED CAPSICUM
- 2 X 250G PUNNETS CHERRY TOMATOES
- 8 CLOVES GARLIC, PEELED
- 1 TSP DRIED THYME
- SALT AND PEPPER
- OLIVE OIL, TO DRIZZLE
- 1 LITRE STOCK (CHICKEN, VEG, BEEF, YOUR CHOICE!)
- 1 TSP CASTER SUGAR
- 300ML POURING CREAM

FOR GIANT CROÛTONS:

- 2 BAGELS
- ¼ CUP OLIVE OIL
- 1 TSP SMOKED PAPRIKA
- ½ TSP GARLIC POWDER
- 1 TSP SALT

WHAT YOU DO

Start off by chopping your red onion and capsicum into pieces about the same size as your cherry tomatoes. We want everyone to play nice together!

Toss the cut onion, capsicum, cherry tomatoes and garlic into a bowl. Sprinkle in the dried thyme. Season the mixture with a bit of salt and pepper, and a drizzle of olive oil.

Now, line the air fryer basket with baking paper and pop this veggie party in! Set the temperature to 200°C and the timer for 20 minutes.

While that's cooking, it's time to prepare your giant croûtons: Split your bagels in half horizontally, then cut each one of those horizontally in half again so you end up with 8 big bagel rounds. In a separate bowl, mix together the olive oil, smoked paprika, garlic powder and salt. Drizzle this tasty mixture over your bagel rounds, making sure they are well covered.

Pop the bagel rounds in the air fryer and set the temperature to 180°C and the timer for 5 minutes.

In the meantime, bring the stock to the boil in a large saucepan.

Once your veggies are air fried to perfection, gently tumble them into your hot stock, then add the sugar and half the cream. Blend this all together using your stick blender until it's lusciously smooth!

Ladle your soup into bowls then use the remaining cream to add a decorative swirl on top. All that's left to do is to pair up each bowl with two giant croûtons.

PREP & COOK TIME 35 mins

STEPH
SAYS
I'M WARNING YOU
NOW, BE PREPARED
TO MAKE MORE GIANT
CROÛTONS BECAUSE
WHO CAN RESIST
THESE CRUNCHY BITS
OF HEAVEN?

SIMPLE CRISPY SKIN SALMON PERFECTION

SERVES 1

WHAT YOU NEED

1 SALMON FILLET, SKIN ON

1 TBSP OLIVE OIL

SALT AND PEPPER

TO SERVE: CRISPY CHUNKY CHIPS (TO MAKE YOUR OWN, SEE PAGE 90)

WHAT YOU DO

Start by patting your salmon dry with some paper towel. This helps to make it super crispy.

Now take that olive oil and give your salmon a nice little massage. Make sure it's covered and happy in that shiny coat. Sprinkle it with salt and pepper. Don't be shy, season so it tastes just right!

Take a piece of baking paper and pop your salmon on it, skin-side up, ready for its hot air journey!

Now, place your salmon in the air fryer. Set the temperature to 200°C and the timer for 7-10 minutes, depending on how well done you like it cooked. If you're a fan of a medium centre, go for 7 minutes. If you like it well done, set it for 10 minutes. And voilà! You've got yourself a delightful crispy skin salmon that will make your taste buds dance! Oh, and don't forget the chips!

PREP & COOK TIME 15 mins

EASY CHEESY CHICKEN RISSOLES

MAKES 14

WHAT YOU NEED

- **1 MEDIUM CARROT**
- **1 MEDIUM ONION**
- **500G CHICKEN MINCE**
- **1½ CUPS GRATED PIZZA CHEESE**
- **½ CUP PANKO BREADCRUMBS**
- **1 TSP GARLIC PASTE**
- **1 TSP SALT**
- **½ TSP PEPPER**
- **OLIVE OIL COOKING SPRAY**

WHAT YOU DO

First up, grate your carrot and onion nice and coarse into a bowl. It's time to mix! Get all the other yummy ingredients into the bowl (except the oil spray) and stir until they're best friends.

Now, let's make them into rissoles. Take ¼ cup of the mix for each and shape into patties. Don't worry about perfection, we love all shapes and sizes!

Let's get your air fryer basket ready. Give it a little spray with some oil.

Pop your lovely little chicken rissoles into the basket and give the tops a bit of a spray too.

Set the temperature to 200°C and the timer for 18 minutes. Turn them over halfway through and give them another little spray with oil. This will give them that gorgeous golden look!

And voilà! You have made some awesome chicken rissoles. If they want a dinner date, you can serve these little lovelies with ketchup and salad, or gravy and my Perfect Chips at Home (page 90) or in brioche buns. The possibilities are endless!

PREP & COOK TIME 25 mins

STEPH
SAYS
ENJOY YOUR
DELICIOUS BUTTER
GARLIC PRAWNS
WITH CRUSTY BREAD
TO SOAK UP EVERY
MORSEL OF THOSE
DELICIOUS JUICES.

SERVES 4

SIZZLING BUTTER GARLIC PRAWNS IN NO TIME!

Buy pre-peeled prawns that are ready to rock 'n' roll for this recipe. I am a fan of the frozen, peeled type with the tails intact, so you can eat this with your fingers.

WHAT YOU NEED

125G SALTED BUTTER

1 TSP GARLIC PASTE

1 SMALL OR ½ LONG RED CHILLI, SEEDS REMOVED, FINELY CHOPPED

SALT AND PEPPER

1 TBSP FINELY CHOPPED PARSLEY

500G GREEN PEELED PRAWNS, READY TO SIZZLE

WHAT YOU DO

Get your air fryer ready by removing the plate from the basket or select a baking dish that will fit.

Time to melt some butter! Put the butter in the bottom of your air fryer basket (or the baking dish) and set the temperature to 160°C and the timer for 2-3 minutes until the butter is all melty.

Now, let's spice things up! Add your garlic, chilli, salt and pepper. Don't forget the parsley! Give it a good stir to mix all those yummy flavours together.

Let's get those prawns in there! Add them to the air fryer basket and make sure they're well coated in that scrumptious butter mix.

Pop the basket back into your air fryer, crank up the heat to 200°C and set the timer for 10 minutes. Remember to give the basket a little shake halfway through to make sure all the prawns are cooking evenly.

PREP & COOK TIME 18 mins

STEPH
SAYS
KEEP A LIL' KITCHEN DIARY! EVERY TIME A DISH ROCKS YOUR WORLD, JOT IT DOWN. OVER TIME, YOU'LL HAVE YOUR VERY OWN COOKBOOK.

SERVES 2

I think the whole world was making this crazy viral dish during lockdown, for good reason – it's quick, easy and delish. In the air fryer it's even faster! You can also throw a bunch of fresh basil in at the end for an extra bang of flavour.

BAKED FETA & TOMATO PASTA AIR-FRYER STYLE

WHAT YOU NEED

- 200G BLOCK OF FETA
- 250G TRUSS CHERRY TOMATOES, SNIPPED INTO LITTLE CLUSTERS
- SALT AND PEPPER
- 1 TSP DRIED CHILLI FLAKES (OPTIONAL)
- ¼ CUP OLIVE OIL
- 175G PENNE, JUST COOKED

WHAT YOU DO

Whip out your trusty air fryer basket and remove the bottom plate or use a baking dish.

Put your feta block right in the centre, like the star it is. Place your tomato clusters around the edge.

Sprinkle over some salt and pepper. Be gentle with the salt though – the feta's got quite a salty personality already!

Got a hankering for a little spice? Add chilli flakes. Pour that olive oil all over. Now, give your dish a little shake-shake; make sure those tomatoes get a nice olive oil bath.

Pop it all into your air fryer, set the temperature to 200°C and the timer for 12 minutes.

Once your feta and tomatoes have had their hot spa treatment, take a fork and gently crush them together. Give them a good mix until you get a beautiful, creamy pink sauce. Looks good, right?

Add your just-cooked pasta into the mix. Give it a good stir and voilà, your baked feta and tomato pasta is ready to be enjoyed!

PREP & COOK TIME 20 mins

SERVES 4

MELT-IN-YOUR-MOUTH HONEY MISO SALMON

If you use the excuse of not knowing how to cook fish for not eating it, then you will no longer be able to say that. This is your new NO FAIL fancy pants salmon recipe!

WHAT YOU NEED

- 1 TBSP HONEY
- 1 TBSP WHITE (SHIRO) MISO
- 1 TBSP SOY SAUCE
- 4 X 200G SKINLESS SALMON FILLETS

WHAT YOU DO

Grab a little bowl and place your honey, white miso and soy sauce in it. Now, it's time to warm up this yummy mix! Pop your bowl into the microwave and heat it up for 30 seconds. Stir everything together to create a deliciously sticky glaze.

Next, dip a pastry brush into your glaze and paint your salmon fillets generously. Make sure every inch is covered with this tasty glaze.

Time to prep your air fryer! Grab some baking paper and line your air fryer basket with it. Now, arrange your salmon fillets on the baking paper with the pretty side facing up. They're ready for their hot air ride!

Set your air fryer temperature to 200°C and the timer for 7-10 minutes, depending on how well done you like your salmon cooked; have a look at Simple Crispy Skin Salmon Perfection over on page 78 for the different timings. Get ready for some delicious, flaky goodness!

PREP & COOK TIME 15 mins

Dinner date Rustle up the Zesty Lemon and Coconut Green Beans, page 71, for a match made in heaven.

STEPH
SAYS
STOP SAYING
"I CAN'T COOK"
IT'S JUST A SKILL
YOU HAVEN'T
LEARNT YET!

STEPH
SAYS
EVERY AIR FRYER
AND PIECE OF FISH
IS DIFFERENT,
SO GIVE YOUR
FISH PARCELS A
QUICK CHECK TO
MAKE SURE THEY
ARE COOKED TO
PERFECTION BEFORE
YOU DIG IN.

MAKES 2

JAZZ UP YOUR DINNER WITH LEMONY BARRAMUNDI PARCELS

If you are looking to impress someone with your cooking expertise, this is the one for you. This not only looks great, but is also very yummy.

WHAT YOU NEED

1 BUNCH BROCCOLINI

2 X 200G BARRAMUNDI FILLETS

SALT AND PEPPER

1 LEMON

100G BUTTER, CHOPPED

WHAT YOU DO

Trim the broccolini stems to roughly match the length of your barramundi fillets. This makes everything nice and neat!

Lay out a large piece of foil and top with a piece of baking paper. They need to be large enough to lovingly wrap up your fish and broccolini. Think of it as a cosy blanket for your ingredients!

Season your barramundi fillets with salt and pepper then place your broccolini in the middle of the baking paper and your fish on top, like they're both ready for a snooze.

Now, slice your lemon into thin rounds. Place 3 lemon slices on top of each barramundi fillet.

Next, place your butter on the lemon. Add a little more salt and pepper for good measure. Butter plus citrus equals delicious!

It's time to wrap up your parcels! Make sure they're secure because we don't want any of those yummy juices to escape. That's liquid gold, my friend!

Remember, it's like wrapping a present: bring the sides of the baking paper up to meet on top, then fold down a few times. Do the same with the ends and tuck them under to keep everything sealed. It's like origami for food!

Pop both your parcels into the air fryer basket and set the temperature to 180°C and the timer for 20 minutes or until your fish is cooked through.

Just like it's Christmas morning, unwrap your delicious parcels!

PREP & COOK TIME 30 mins

MAKES 16

FLAVOUR-PACKED ITALIAN MEATBALLS

Now, sit back, relax, and get ready for the aroma of Italian cuisine to fill your kitchen. Pop these meatballs over spaghetti and you will be loving yourself sick!

WHAT YOU NEED

- 500G PORK AND VEAL MINCE BLEND
- ¼ CUP MILK
- ½ CUP PANKO BREADCRUMBS
- ¼ CUP DICED BACON
- 1 TSP FENNEL SEEDS
- ¼ CUP FINELY GRATED PARMESAN
- 1 TBSP TOMATO PASTE
- 2 TBSP CHOPPED PARSLEY
- 1 TSP SALT
- ½ TSP PEPPER
- OLIVE OIL COOKING SPRAY
- 700ML BOTTLE TOMATO PASSATA
- TO SERVE: COOKED SPAGHETTI AND EXTRA PARMESAN

WHAT YOU DO

First, grab a big bowl and pop in your pork and veal mince, the milk, breadcrumbs, bacon, fennel seeds, parmesan, tomato paste, parsley, salt and pepper.

Now, get in there with your hands and mix it up until it's nice and combined!

Once that's done, roll the mixture into balls about the size of a golf ball.

Now, let's get your air fryer ready! Spray it with a bit of olive oil and place your meatballs in a single layer inside. Spray the tops of the meatballs with some more olive oil.

Time to cook! Set the temperature to 200°C and the timer for 10 minutes, but don't forget to turn them halfway through and give them another spritz of olive oil.

After 10 minutes, take out your meatballs and remove the plate at the bottom of your air fryer basket. You can also use a baking pan or dish that fits your fryer if that works better for you.

Place your meatballs back in the basket and pour over the bottle of tomato passata.

Put it back in your air fryer. Set the temperature again to 200°C and the timer for 20 minutes, giving it all a good ol' stir halfway through. Then it's just a matter of serving it all with bowls of spaghetti and more parmesan.

PREP & COOK TIME 45 mins

STEPH
SAYS
DON'T HAVE
THAT SPECIFIC
INGREDIENT?
IMPROVISE!
SOMETIMES THE BEST
DISHES COME FROM
THINKING OUTSIDE
THE RECIPE BOX.

SERVES 4

SIMPLE STEPS TO PERFECT CHIPS AT HOME

Yes these chips are already perfect, but why not take them up a notch with a trip around the world of spices. You'll find 4 seriously good seasonings on page 93 to choose from!

WHAT YOU NEED

500G POTATOES

1 TBSP CORNFLOUR

1 TSP SALT

½ TSP PEPPER

1 TSP SWEET PAPRIKA (FOR A FUN SPLASH OF COLOUR, BUT TOTALLY UP TO YOU)

OLIVE OIL COOKING SPRAY

WHAT YOU DO

Whether you're on team peel or team no-peel, decide on the fate of your potatoes. I usually keep the skins on!

Cut those potatoes into 1cm-thick chips. Think about the joy of that perfect crunch as you do!

Give your chips a cold water bath. Drain, rinse and pat them dry. They'll thank you later, promise!

Toss the chips in a bowl with the combined cornflour, salt, pepper and paprika until they're all glammed up.

Now, off to the air fryer they go. Spray them nicely with some oil. They're ready for their hot air!

Set your air fryer temperature to 200°C and the timer for 25 minutes, but don't forget to give them a good shake every 5 minutes until they are golden brown. It's like their own little dance party!

After 25 minutes, they're all done! Sprinkle with a bit more salt and pepper if you like. Bon appétit!

PREP & COOK TIME 35 mins

STEPH SAYS

WHEN I SAY GOLDEN BROWN, I REALLY MEAN THE DARKEST YOU CAN GET JUST BEFORE IT'S BURNT. TRUST ME, IT'S LIFE-CHANGING!

SERIOUSLY GOOD

SHAKER SEASONINGS

WHAT YOU DO Choose one of my dynamite-yummo flavoured salts opposite then combine the ingredients in a small bowl. Next, make Simple Steps to the Perfect Chips at Home (page 90), leving out the paprika. Now for the fun part – place your chip creations in a large bowl, then sprinkle over the flavoured salt and get shakin' to combine your seasoning magic.

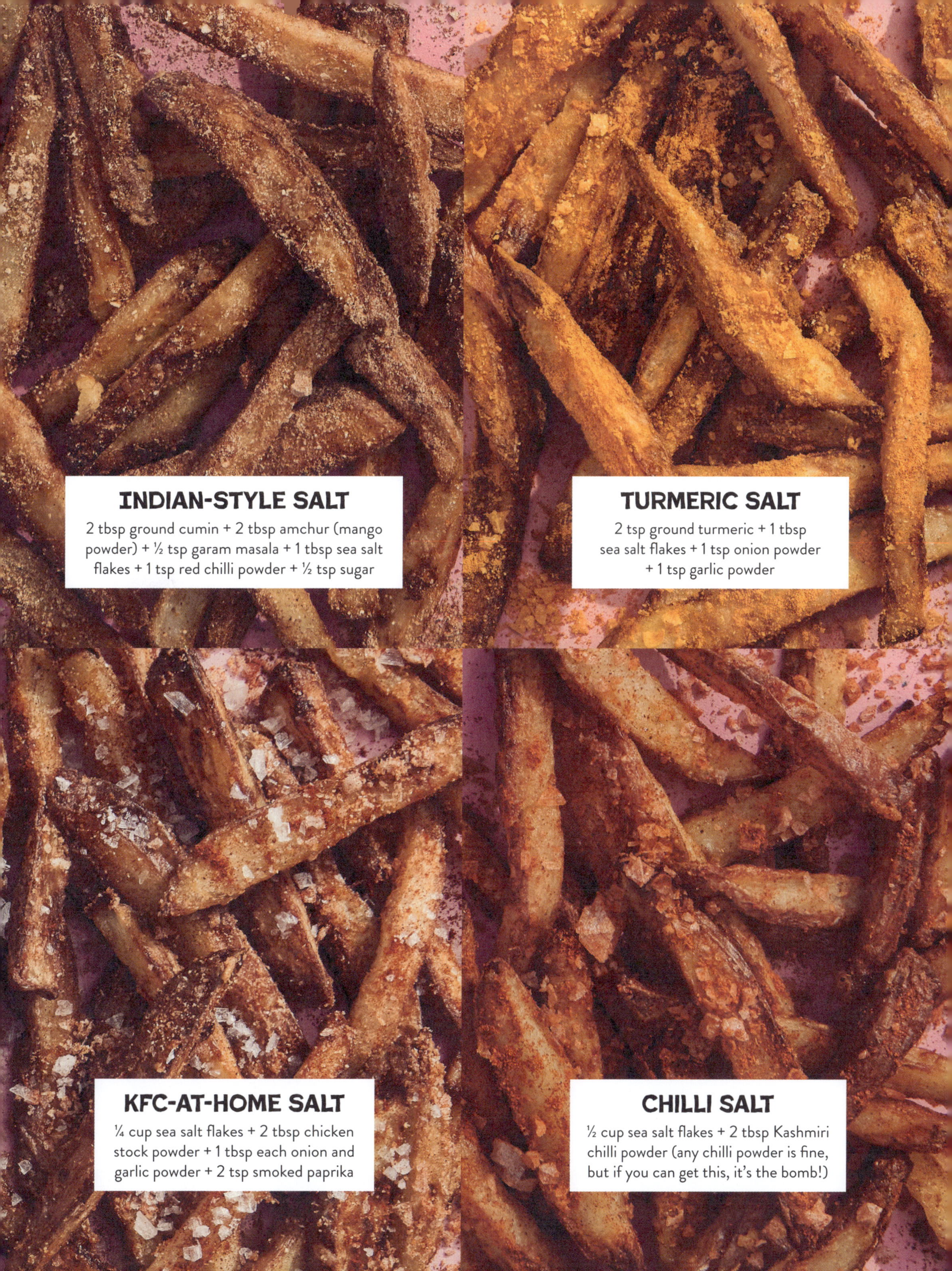

INDIAN-STYLE SALT

2 tbsp ground cumin + 2 tbsp amchur (mango powder) + ½ tsp garam masala + 1 tbsp sea salt flakes + 1 tsp red chilli powder + ½ tsp sugar

TURMERIC SALT

2 tsp ground turmeric + 1 tbsp sea salt flakes + 1 tsp onion powder + 1 tsp garlic powder

KFC-AT-HOME SALT

¼ cup sea salt flakes + 2 tbsp chicken stock powder + 1 tbsp each onion and garlic powder + 2 tsp smoked paprika

CHILLI SALT

½ cup sea salt flakes + 2 tbsp Kashmiri chilli powder (any chilli powder is fine, but if you can get this, it's the bomb!)

DIRTY DESSERTS

MAKES 6

SPRING INTO APPLE PIE

Even an apple pie deserves a spring glow up. Spring roll wrapper meets juicy filling, all crisped to perfection in the air fryer. Sweet, crispy, irresistible!

WHAT YOU NEED

- **385G CAN APPLE SLICES PIE FRUIT**
- **1 TBSP BROWN SUGAR**
- **1 TSP CORNFLOUR**
- **6 SPRING ROLL WRAPPERS, THAWED**
- **OLIVE OIL COOKING SPRAY**
- **60G BUTTER, MELTED**
- **⅓ CUP CINNAMON SUGAR**
- **TO SERVE: VANILLA ICE-CREAM AND TOASTED FLAKED ALMONDS**

WHAT YOU DO

In a bowl, mix together the apples, brown sugar and cornflour.

Grab a spring roll wrapper and lay it flat. Scoop up ⅓ cup of your apple mix and pop it right on top of your wrapper in a line, a little bit up from the bottom.

Rollin' time! Fold the sides in and roll it up, making sure all that yummy filling stays inside. Dab a bit of water on the edge to seal it up all nice and tight.

Now they're all rolled up. Give them a little spray with olive oil spray and pop them in the air fryer. Remember, just one layer at a time.

Set the temperature to 200°C and the timer for 7 minutes and fry those beauties until they turn a lovely golden brown. Flip 'em, give another spritz of cooking spray, and repeat air frying for another 5 minutes.

Once they're all crispy and golden, roll them in the melted butter, then in the cinnamon sugar while they're still hot. Mmm, can you smell that?

Serve these crispy rolls with a scoop of ice-cream (or two!) and a shower of toasted almonds.

PREP & COOK TIME 20 mins

STEPH
SAYS
EVERY GREAT COOK
WAS ONCE A BEGINNER
WHO USED SALT
INSTEAD OF SUGAR.

STEPH
SAYS
ENJOY THIS CRUMBLE
WITH A DOLLOP OF
FRESH CREAM OR A
SCOOP OF VANILLA
ICE-CREAM AND A
CARAMEL DRIZZLE.

SERVES 6

Dive into the ultimate dessert: my unbeatable anything crumble. Sweet, crunchy and perfection in every bite! The best part, you choose your own fruit adventure.

UNBEATABLE ANYTHING CRUMBLE

WHAT YOU NEED

- **2 X 410G CANS APPLES, PEACHES, APRICOTS OR 500G FROZEN BERRIES**
- **1 TBSP CORNFLOUR**
- **1 TSP GROUND CINNAMON**
- **250G BUTTER, MELTED**
- **1 CUP ROLLED OATS**
- **1 CUP SHREDDED COCONUT**
- **1 CUP PLAIN FLOUR**
- **1 CUP FIRMLY PACKED BROWN SUGAR**

WHAT YOU DO

Take out the bottom plate of your air fryer or grab a 5-cup baking pan that fits your fryer. Empty the cans of fruit (including the syrup if using peaches or apricots) or place berries in it. Sprinkle the cornflour and cinnamon over the fruit. Give everything a good mix, making sure all the fruit is well coated. Once done, set it aside for a while.

In a separate bowl, put in the melted butter, oats, coconut, flour and sugar. Stir everything together until it's well mixed and forms clumps.

Sprinkle the crumble mixture over the top of your fruit. But, don't press it down, you want to keep it a bit chunky. That way, you end up with some deliciously big chunks of crumble bits.

Pop your crumble into your air fryer, set the temperature to 180°C and the timer for 15 minutes. Your delightful air fryer crumble is ready to serve.

PREP & COOK TIME 25 mins

MAKES 30

ANYTIME CHOCOLATE CHIP COOKIES

You will be banging these little treasures out every weekend as the dough only takes 5 minutes to put together, though they do need extra chill time in the fridge and bake time.

WHAT YOU NEED

- 2½ CUPS PLAIN FLOUR
- 1 CUP FIRMLY PACKED BROWN SUGAR
- ½ CUP CASTER SUGAR
- 1 TSP BAKING POWDER
- 2 EXTRA-LARGE EGGS
- 200G BUTTER, MELTED
- A SPLASH OF VANILLA
- 250G DARK CHOCOLATE CHIPS
- OLIVE OIL COOKING SPRAY

WHAT YOU DO

Mix together the plain flour, sugars and baking powder until they're all good friends.

Now, let's add the eggs, melted butter, that splash of vanilla and those chocolate chips to the party. Stir everything up!

Got everything mixed? Awesome! Now, let's shape this dough into a neat 36cm long log and about 5cm in diameter, then wrap it nice and tight in some baking paper.

Give the dough a little rest in the fridge for about 1 hour.

Time to let the cookie dough breathe! After chilling, unwrap the whole log and cut it into yummy cookie-sized slices, about 1cm thick.

Spray your air fryer basket with oil then place 5 cookies about 4cm apart into your basket. Set the temperature to 160°C and the timer for 7 minutes. Keep an eye on them as you don't want any crispy critters!

Let them cool for a few minutes before taking them out of the air fryer. Repeat with the remaining cookies four more times.

PREP & COOK TIME
1 hour (+ refrigeration)

STEPH
SAYS
EVERY AIR FRYER IS DIFFERENT SO COOKING THESE COOKIES AT A SLIGHTLY LOWER TEMPERATURE IS A DANCE MOVE THAT'LL KEEP THEM FROM OVER-BROWNING!

Gudbud

During school holidays we have a family tradition, that includes games of backyard putt putt, a crazy course created with things out of our garage, finished with a Gudbud. Traditionally, gudbud is an ice-cream sundae served with scoops of ice-cream, bits of mango, cubes of jelly and nuts. But ours has evolved, as all great things do. It's now a mash up of chocolate cake (page 120), vanilla ice-cream with crushed chocolate chip cookies (page 100), marshmallows, and whatever else we can think of!

Ice Cream
Ice Cream

Ice Cream
Ice Cream

STEPH
SAYS
TRY AND STOP AT
EATING JUST ONE OF
THESE! SET THE TIMER
FOR 2 MINUTES LESS
THAN THE RECIPE, AND
CHECK THEY AREN'T
OVER-BROWNING!

MAKES 20

THE WEET-BIX SLICE THAT'LL STEAL THE SHOW

This crunchy, chocolatey delight will have you wondering why you forgot about this one from your misspent youth. There is a reason these old-school recipes are making a comeback!

WHAT YOU NEED

- 3 WEET-BIX
- ½ CUP CASTER SUGAR
- 1 CUP SELF-RAISING FLOUR
- 1 CUP DESICCATED COCONUT
- 2 TBSP COCOA POWDER
- 150G BUTTER, CHOPPED

FOR THE TOPPING:

- 2 CUPS ICING SUGAR
- 1½ TBSP COCOA POWDER
- 1 TBSP SOFTENED BUTTER
- 2 TSP DESICCATED COCONUT

WHAT YOU DO

Smash those Weet-Bix! Get 'em all crushed in a bowl. Add in your dry buddies: sugar, flour, coconut and cocoa. Give it a good ol' stir.

Time to get buttery! Melt that butter in the microwave in 15-second bursts and mix it into your bowl of dry stuff.

Grease then line a 20cm square cake pan with baking paper. Dump your mix into the pan and press it down like you mean it. Use the back of a spoon to get it even and firm.

Pop it in the air fryer and set the temperature to 160°C and the timer for 20 minutes.

While the base gets all crispy, whip up that topping: combine icing sugar, cocoa, butter and 2-3 tablespoons water until you get a thick icing.

Slather the topping over the base while it's hot, then sprinkle on the coconut. Let it chill out in the fridge and cool down completely in the pan.

Lift that beautiful slice out and cut it up into 20 yummy pieces.

PREP & COOK TIME
30 mins (+ cooling)

MAKES 10

Choose your own adventure with these bars. Make them as healthy or indulgent as you like. FYI, I soaked the dried cranberries in hot water for 5 mins so they didn't shrivel during the cook.

NUTTY DELIGHT MUESLI BARS

WHAT YOU NEED

½ CUP SUPER SMOOTH PEANUT BUTTER

2 TBSP HONEY

1½ CUPS ROLLED OATS

1 EXTRA-LARGE EGG

1 CUP OF ADD-INS (CHOCOLATE CHIPS, DRIED CRANBERRIES, NUTS – WHATEVER MAKES YOUR TASTE BUDS DANCE!)

WHAT YOU DO

In a microwave-safe bowl, stir together your peanut butter and honey. Heat this duo in the microwave for about 1 minute or until they melt into a deliciously gooey mix. Give it a nice stir.

Time to gather the gang! Add in the oats, egg and your chosen add-ins to the bowl. Mix, mix, mix until everything's combined. It's like a mini arm workout!

Grease then line a 20cm square cake pan with baking paper. Spoon in your mixture, spread it evenly and give it a firm press.

Put the pan in the air fryer and set the temperature to 160°C and the timer for 20 minutes.

Once it's done, let it cool down to room temperature, then cut into 10 bars.

Voilà! Munch away on your delightful homemade muesli bars!

PREP & COOK TIME
30 mins (+ cooling)

STEPH SAYS
BRUSH THE TOP WITH A LITTLE HONEY TO MAKE THESE BEAUTIES GLOSSY, THEN POP INTO AN AIRTIGHT CONTAINER AND KEEP FOR UP TO 1 WEEK.

STEPH
SAYS
THE GREAT THING ABOUT THIS SLICE IS IT'S JUST AS GREAT AFTER A WEEK AS IT IS THE DAY IT WAS MADE. JUST KEEP IT IN THE FRIDGE!

MAKES 16

Remember the good ol' days of passionfruit vines growing wild in our yards? Ours took over the chook shed! Fresh is great, but those cute little supermarket cans are a total game-changer for this recipe.

YOUR NEW FAVOURITE PASSIONFRUIT SLICE!

WHAT YOU NEED

- **1 CUP SELF-RAISING FLOUR**
- **1 CUP DESICCATED COCONUT**
- **½ CUP CASTER SUGAR**
- **125G BUTTER, MELTED**
- **ICING SUGAR, TO DUST**
- **FOR THE YUMMY TOPPING:**
- **395G CAN SWEETENED CONDENSED MILK**
- **4 PASSIONFRUIT, PULP REMOVED**

WHAT YOU DO

In a large mixing bowl, stir together the flour, coconut, sugar and melted butter until combined.

Grease then line a 20cm square cake pan with baking paper. Press all the mixture into your pan, make sure it's evenly spread.

Place it in the air fryer and set the temperature to 160°C and the timer for 15 minutes. It'll start to turn a lovely golden colour.

While that's baking, in a separate bowl, mix the yummy topping ingredientss: sweetened condensed milk and passionfruit pulp. Once your base is baked, pour that delightful passionfruit mixture right over the top.

Send it back to the air fryer, keep the temperature at 160°C and set the timer for 10 minutes.

Once it's done, let it cool to room temperature.

Lastly, dust that beauty with a little icing sugar, then cut into mouth-watering squares and serve. Enjoy your tropical delight!

PREP & COOK TIME 35 mins

MAKES 20

Ever had a combo so unexpectedly delicious, you'd swear it's sorcery? This 3-ingredient wonder defies all logic. Not only does it taste out of this world, but it also gives a cheeky wink to the scone rules the purists preach!!

MAGIC 3-INGREDIENT SCONES

WHAT YOU NEED

3½ CUPS SELF-RAISING FLOUR, PLUS EXTRA TO DUST

1 CUP THICKENED CREAM

1 CUP LEMONADE

WHAT YOU DO

Grab a big bowl and tip your flour in it. Create a little hollow in the middle – that's where the fun stuff will go!

Pour your thickened cream and lemonade into that hollow. Now, get that spatula and stir it all together. What you're aiming for is a sticky ball of dough, but be gentle, we want to keep those lemonade bubbles alive as this will make the scones light.

Time to get a bit messy! Dust your bench top with a little extra flour and dump the dough on top. Remember to be gentle; next, gently pat out the dough with your hands until it is about 2.5cm thick. We're not going for neat here. The less you touch them the better your scones will be.

Got a scone cutter? Awesome! Use it to cut out as many scones as you can. Or just use a knife and have square scones, they taste just as good. Press the leftovers together and go again.

Now, line the air fryer basket with baking paper and pop in 16 of your scones, side-by-side, into 4 rows of 4.

Set the temperature to 170°C and the timer for 12 minutes and wait for the magic to happen. Once they're a beautiful golden colour they're done! Repeat with the remaining 4 scones.

PREP & COOK TIME 40 mins

STEPH
SAYS
NOW ALL YOU
NEED TO DECIDE,
IS IF THE JAM OR
THE CREAM GOES
ON THE BOTTOM?

STEPH
SAYS
IF YOU WANT TO MAKE
CARAMEL CAKIES,
USE CARAMILK CHIPS.

MAKES 20

CORNFLAKE CAKIES YOU NEED TO MAKE!

Cakies alert! These treats are the best of both worlds – they've got the softness of a cake inside and that cornflake crunch outside. Not quite a cake, not quite a cookie… it's a Cakie!

WHAT YOU NEED

125G BUTTER, SOFTENED

½ CUP CASTER SUGAR

1 EXTRA-LARGE EGG

1 CUP DARK CHOCOLATE CHIPS

1 CUP SELF-RAISING FLOUR

¾ CUP CORNFLAKES, CRUSHED

OLIVE OIL COOKING SPRAY

WHAT YOU DO

In a small bowl, stir the butter and sugar until they're looking all smooth and dreamy. No machines needed here folks!

Time to welcome the egg into the mix! Beat it all in until everyone is happy together.

Now, let's add some sweetness and crunch. Stir in the chocolate chips and flour until the mixture is like a soft dough.

Take rounded tablespoons of our yummy mixture, roll them in the crushed cornflakes. It's like giving them a crunchy little jacket!

Spray your air fryer basket with oil and pop in 4 of your soon-to-be-cakies, 4cm apart, and give them a little pat to flatten them slightly.

Time to bake! Set the air fryer temperature to 160°C and the timer for 8 minutes. You'll know they're done when they turn a lovely shade of golden brown.

Give them a moment to cool down a bit before you take them out. Patience, my friend! They're worth the wait. Then repeat the process with the remaining mixture in four more batches.

PREP & COOK TIME 55 mins

MAKES 2 (EACH FEEDS 6)

You have to just trust me with this one, you have to burn it. I know you think I have lost the plot but just trust the process. The burnt top honestly makes this Basque cheesecake so delicious.

TWO BURNT CHEESECAKES

WHAT YOU NEED

750G CREAM CHEESE, SOFTENED

1½ CUPS CASTER SUGAR

A GOOD PINCH OF SALT

5 EXTRA-LARGE EGGS

¾ CUP THICKENED CREAM

A SPLASH OF VANILLA

WHAT YOU DO

Toss everything into your trusty food processor or blender. Give it a whirl until it's looking super smooth. Be patient, this will take a few minutes!

Grab two 17cm (6-cup) round cake pans, or you could use two 15.7cm x 21.9cm (4cm deep) disposable aluminium trays, then line them with baking paper.

Share the creamy mix between the two pans. Half in one, half in the other.

Pop one of the pans into the air fryer and set the temperature to 200°C and the timer for 25-30 minutes; you're looking for a gentle wobble in the middle and a very dark brown top.

Once that's done, take the basket out of the air fryer, then leave your cheesecake creation in there to cool for about 5 minutes.

Repeat the process with your second dreamy cheesecake.

For the best flavour, let your cheesecakes chill in the fridge for a few hours.

When you're ready, slice up your cheesecakes and serve. These little beauties can also be frozen for up to 1 month.

PREP & COOK TIME
1 hour 10 mins (+ cooling)

STEPH
SAYS
IF YOU DON'T NEED TO SERVE BOTH CHEESECAKES AT THE SAME TIME, COVER THE SECOND ONE AND POP IT IN THE FRIDGE TO COOK THE NEXT DAY.

STEPH
SAYS
WHEN LIFE HANDS
YOU LEMONS, SWAP
OUT THE ORANGE
ZEST AND JUICE FOR
LEMON FRESHNESS.

SERVES 8

If orange isn't your jam, you can turn this into a zesty lemon, luscious lime or magic mandarin cake by subbing out the oranges with your favourite citrus.

ORANGE BLISS TEA CAKE

WHAT YOU NEED

- 125G BUTTER, MELTED
- ¾ CUP CASTER SUGAR
- 3 EXTRA-LARGE EGGS
- GRATED ZEST OF 2 ORANGES
- 2 TBSP ORANGE JUICE
- 2 TBSP DESICCATED COCONUT
- 1 CUP SELF-RAISING FLOUR
- TO SERVE: VANILLA YOGHURT, SLIVERED PISTACHIOS AND HONEY

WHAT YOU DO

Start by whisking the melted butter, sugar, eggs and that fresh orange zest and juice together in a bowl until it's all mixed up and happy.

Time to make it even yummier! Add the coconut and flour. Give it a good stir until everything's best buddies.

Grab a 20cm square or round cake pan, grease then line it with baking paper. Once you're all set, pour the batter into your pan. Let's get to baking! Pop it into your air fryer.

Set the temperature to 150°C and the timer for 30-35 minutes. To check it's done, pop a skewer into the centre and pull it out; the cake should be dry to the touch.

When it's done, cool it slightly before lifting it out of the pan. You should have a delightful treat that's golden and scrumptious!

Cut the cake into 8 slices. Eat it as it is or make it fancy with a dollop of yoghurt, some little jewels of green pistachio and a drizzle of honey lusciousness.

PREP & COOK TIME 45 mins

MAKES 8

If you are a coffee hater, then I don't think we can be friends, but you can still make this cake. Just swap the coffee for chocolate, warm milk or cream.

CAFFEINATED CHOCOLATE CAKES

WHAT YOU NEED

- ½ CUP HOT COFFEE
- ½ CUP MILK
- A DASH OF VANILLA
- 1 EXTRA-LARGE EGG
- 60G BUTTER, MELTED
- 1 CUP SELF-RAISING FLOUR
- ¼ TSP BICARBONATE OF SODA
- ½ CUP COCOA POWDER
- 1 CUP CASTER SUGAR
- ½ CUP CHOCOLATE CHIPS

FOR THE ICING:

- 2 CUPS ICING SUGAR
- 1 TBSP SOFTENED BUTTER
- 2 TBSP MILK

WHAT YOU DO

In a bowl, whisk together your wet ingredients. Start with the hot coffee, milk and vanilla, then whisk in the egg and melted butter. Give it a good mix until they're all smooth and friendly with each other.

Time for the dry team! Add in the self-raising flour, bicarb, cocoa and sugar. Stir it all up until you have a lovely, smooth batter. Finally, stir in all those little chocolate chips.

Grease and line the base of 8 x 1-cup baking moulds with baking paper. Pour the chocolatey magic mixture into each mould (about ¼ cup for each one) – yes, it's supposed to look that yummy!

Time to air fry! Place 4 of the moulds in your air fryer basket. Set the temperature to 150°C and the timer for 20 minutes. They're cooked when you pop a wooden skewer into the middle of one and it comes out dry.

Repeat the process with the other 4 moulds.

Now imagine the deliciousness you are about to enjoy.

While your cakes are cooking, make your icing: stir the icing sugar and butter together, adding the milk 1 tablespoon at a time, until it's all smooth and drizzly.

Turn your cakes out onto a rack and spoon over your icing.

Now, if you want to make just one big cake, grease and line an 11.5cm x 21.5cm loaf pan (don't forget to make sure it fits in your air fryer!). You'll need to cook it for 40-45 minutes.

PREP & COOK TIME 45 mins

STEPH
SAYS
ANY OL' COFFEE
WILL DO: ESPRESSO
OR INSTANT –
YOU CHOOSE.

BLUEBERRY CHEESECAKE

60g softened cream cheese + 1 tbsp caster sugar + 1 tsp ground cinnamon + 1 cup blueberries + zest of 1 lemon

OH-SO-EASY!

POCKET PIES

MAKES 4

Cut 2 sheets thawed puff pastry into 8 squares (that's 4 from each sheet). Top 4 of your squares with your chosen filling, layering them in the order listed. Sandwich with remaining pastry squares, sealing your little pockets so there are no escapees. Paint them with beaten egg. Spray the air fryer basket with olive oil. Place your pies in the basket in 2 batches. Set the temperature to 200°C and the timer for 7 minutes. Turn the pies over and cook them for a further 3 minutes or until golden and crispy. Let them cool slightly, then dust with icing sugar snow.

PREP & COOK TIME 25 mins

STRAWBERRIES & CREAM
½ cup firm ricotta + 125g sliced strawberries + ½ tsp grated orange zest + 1 tbsp vanilla sugar
LEMON CUSTARD
Custard (below) + ⅓ cup lemon curd + 2 tbsp slivered pistachios
For custard: Mix 1½ tbsp custard powder + 2 tsp caster sugar + 1 cup milk. Microwave 2 mins, stirring halfway, stir again. Chill custard.
GOOEY S'MORES
⅓ cup Nutella + ⅓ cup Biscoff spread + ½ cup mini marshmallows

STEPH
SAYS
CHOOSE ANOTHER MARMALADE FOR YOUR OWN FLAVOUR-TWIST ADVENTURE.

SERVES 4

I am a sucker for a bread pudding, but if you use brioche, add chocolate chips and orange marmalade like I did to this one, you all of a sudden turn it from Grandma's pudding to a hip dessert.

GROWN-UP JAFFA BREAD PUDDING

WHAT YOU NEED

4 CUPS (140G) CUBED BRIOCHE

¼ CUP ORANGE MARMALADE

½ CUP DARK CHOCOLATE CHIPS

FOR THE CUSTARD:

2 EXTRA-LARGE EGGS

1 CUP MILK

½ CUP POURING CREAM

2 TBSP CASTER SUGAR

A SPLASH OF VANILLA

A PINCH OF SALT

TO SERVE: ICING SUGAR TO DUST

WHAT YOU DO

Start off by whisking together all the ingredients for the custard in a large bowl; that's the eggs, milk, cream, sugar, vanilla and a little pinch of salt. Go on, get them all friendly with each other.

Now, invite your brioche cubes to the party! Gently stir them around in the custard to make sure each piece gets coated in the creamy goodness.

Get ready for action! Grease a 16cm x 20cm baking dish or pan that will fit your air fryer.

Take half of your custard-soaked brioche cubes and lay them out on the base of your baking dish.

Drop spoonfuls of marmalade over the brioche, then rain half the chocolate chips over the top.

Layer over the remaining soaked brioche cubes. Make sure you cover up all the marmalade and chocolate spots as, trust me, you don't want those to burn.

Pour over any leftover custard mix from the bowl.

Ready to bake? Place the baking dish in the air fryer and set the temperature to 160°C and the timer for 15 minutes; the pudding is done when the custard is set with a slight wobble.

Scatter over the rest of the chocolate chips and dust with icing sugar.

PREP & COOK TIME 30 mins

CONVERSION CHART

MEASURES

One Australian metric measuring cup holds approximately 250ml; one Australian metric tablespoon holds 20ml; one Australian metric teaspoon holds 5ml. The difference between one country's measuring cups and another's is within a two- or three-teaspoon variance and will not affect your cooking results. North America, New Zealand and the United Kingdom use a 15ml tablespoon. All cup and spoon measurements are level.

The most accurate way of measuring dry ingredients is to weigh them.

When measuring liquids, use a clear glass or plastic jug with the metric markings.

We use extra-large eggs with an average weight of 60g each.

DRY MEASURES

metric	imperial
15g	½oz
30g	1oz
60g	2oz
90g	3oz
125g	4oz (¼lb)
155g	5oz
185g	6oz
220g	7oz
250g	8oz (½lb)
280g	9oz
315g	10oz
345g	11oz
375g	12oz (¾lb)
410g	13oz
440g	14oz
470g	15oz
500g	16oz (1lb)
750g	24oz (1½lb)
1kg	32oz (2lb)

LIQUID MEASURES

metric	imperial
30ml	1 fluid oz
60ml	2 fluid oz
100ml	3 fluid oz
125ml	4 fluid oz
150ml	5 fluid oz
190ml	6 fluid oz
250ml	8 fluid oz
300ml	10 fluid oz
500ml	16 fluid oz
600ml	20 fluid oz
1000ml (1 litre)	1¾ pints

LENGTH MEASURES

metric	imperial
3mm	⅛in
6mm	¼in
1cm	½in
2cm	¾in
2.5cm	1in
5cm	2in
6cm	2½in
8cm	3in
10cm	4in
13cm	5in
15cm	6in
18cm	7in
20cm	8in
22cm	9in
25cm	10in
28cm	11in
30cm	12in (1ft)

OVEN TEMPERATURES

The temperatures below are for conventional ovens; for fan-forced temperatures, you will need to decrease the temperature by 10-20 degrees.

	°C (Celsius)	°F (Fahrenheit)
Very slow	100	210
Slow	130	260
Moderately slow	140	280
Moderate	160	325
Moderately hot	180	350
Hot	200	400
Very hot	220	425

Measurements for cake pans are approximate only. Using same-shaped cake pans of a similar size should not affect the outcome of your baking. We measure the inside top of the cake pan to determine size.

INDEX

are
media books

ARE MEDIA
Chief executive officer Jane Huxley

ARE MEDIA BOOKS
General manager Nicole Byers
Editorial & food director Sophia Young
Books director David Scotto
Creative director & designer Hannah Blackmore
Managing editor Stephanie Kistner
Food editor Sophia Young
Production controller Kara Stead

Author Steph de Sousa

FOOD
Photographer Alana Landsberry
Photochef Rebecca Lyall
Stylist Kate Brown
Props stylist Olivia Blackmore

COVER & LIFESTYLE
Photographer Alana Landsberry
Stylist Kate Brown
Hair & makeup Allison Boyle

Printed in China by Leo Paper Products.

A catalogue record for this book is available from the National Library of Australia.
ISBN 978-1-76122-178-1

Published by Are Media Books, a division of Are Media Pty Limited, 54 Park St, Sydney; GPO Box 4088, Sydney, NSW 2001, Australia
Ph +61 2 9282 8000
www.aremediabooks.com.au

Published in 2024 by Are Media Books, Australia.
Are Media Books is a division of Are Media Pty Ltd.